Community Life 101

Getting the Most Out of Your Small Group Experience

By Randall Neighbour

Published by Cell Group Resources
10055 Regal Row, Suite 180
Houston, Texas 77040 USA
(713) 896-7478 • Fax (713) 896-1874

Cover and illustrations by Don Bleyl

International Standard Book Number: 0-9752896-2-4

Cell Group Resources is a book-publishing division of
TOUCH Outreach Ministries, Inc., a resource, training and
consulting ministry for churches with a vision for holistic
small group or cell-based local church structure.

Find us on the web at: www.cellgrouppeople.com

To send the author feedback, email:
randall@cellgrouppeople.com

Acknowledgements

If it were not for the following people, this book would never be in your hands . . .

Etna, words cannot express what a wonderful co-laborer in small group ministry you are! It's great to be married to my very best friend.

Scott, thank you for challenging me to write and more importantly, re-write this book.

Robbi, thanks for making me look so good with your clear understanding of the English language and your excellent proofing skills.

Mark, thank you for the excellent feedback you provided. May God richly bless your work at Faith Promise, Knoxville.

Thank you, my dear friends in my current and past small groups, for the incredible times of joy we've had together as we've built the kingdom of God.

Table of Contents

Introduction

When I was a kid, Christmas morning was hands-down the best day of the year. For weeks leading up to this wonderful day, I dreamed of unwrapping that special toy. In the mind of a child, Christmas Day was all about receiving gifts.

December 25th is still one of the best days of the year! As an adult, I now receive a great deal of joy and satisfaction knowing I have found the perfect gift for my wife, family, or friends. Now it's all about giving, just like the reason for the season...the gift of Jesus Christ, our Savior.

It may be that your main objective in small group life is to discover what you can get out of it, which isn't a bad place to start. I think everyone looks at something new and thinks about this first.

Your small group offers a lot, including a sense of belonging, and a place to discover God and share one's hurts. But just like my shift in thinking about Christmas, you'll find that the more you invest in others, the better group life becomes for you.

This book was purposely designed to be brief and lighthearted. Others have written deep, theological books on the basis of community. I've read many of these books and none of them told me how to be a better small group member or get more out of it. That's why I wrote this book, and filled it with true stories from my life in small groups. I hope you enjoy it, and find a bunch of good tips and ideas to make your small group the best thing in which you've ever been a part!

A Quick Note: At the end of each chapter, you'll find some practical ways you can apply and share what you've read. If the chapter leaves you wanting more, additional resources are listed.

Chapter 1
What is Biblical Community?

I grew up in the church as a preacher's kid. Life was my church and church was my life. My dad, the senior pastor, ensured our church always had a very strong small group emphasis that included prayer, ministry to one another, and lots of time invested in unchurched people.

By the time I was a junior in high school, I was a successful small group leader in our church's growing youth group. Seven of my friends found Christ that year and four of them became group leaders themselves. This small group experience, or what I would call my Christian community, gave me a strong sense of purpose in life during my difficult adolescent years.

Being a small group leader in high school was exciting. I saw God radically change my friends and even their parents, who wanted to know what had transformed their teenagers. Despite all the good I saw and experienced, I still longed to be on my own and independent from family and church. I couldn't find where my family and church ended and my personal faith began.

I stopped going to church when I left home and enrolled in a Christian college. I decided that five days of chapel every week was enough church for anyone. I dropped out of college in 1982, moved back home, and took a job in a small, independent photography lab near downtown Houston, far away from my childhood home and church in the suburbs.

One day, the owner of a little tavern down the street came into my photo lab to have his vacation pictures developed. He invited my boss and me to come to his bar after work for a beer. He said that if we showed up, he'd buy the first round because we did such a great job on his pictures.

When my boss and I walked in that evening, we both were definitely outside our comfort zones. The tavern was dumpy; it smelled a little; the carpet was nasty; and the clientele actually scared me. It just looked like one of those places in the movies where the bikers start fights over side-glances at their girlfriends.

From my Baptist upbringing, this would be considered the exact *opposite* of church, right up there with topless bars, casinos, and pawn shops. (Don't ask me why pawn shops were considered bad places, but they were!) The bar owner introduced us to his wife and a couple of regulars in the bar. He told them that we made him look like a professional photographer, and everyone should take their film down to our lab when they get home from vacation. This was music to my boss' ears—he was desperate for more customers!

My boss had a beer and I had a cup of coffee, mostly because growing up as a preacher's kid, I never drank alcohol. The bar owner's wife thought my request for coffee was hilarious, and she told me she'd give me a free cup of coffee anytime I wanted to come in for a "drink."

This was music to my ears. I was broke and starved for community—the kind I had in high school in my small group. Her offer was all I needed to become a regular at this dump every day at lunch and most evenings after work. (She fed me often for what I had in my pocket that day.)

Since I was not in a church where I could find community, this dump became a place of community for me. Everyone knew one another and helped out when someone had car trouble or needed a ride home. The regulars in this bar listened to each other's problems even though they couldn't do much to solve what was shared. I always thought, "What if church could be just like this place, with the addition of worship and an understanding of the love of God?"

Six years after my high school graduation, I came back to the church through an invitation from a high school friend. He said he'd found a church where their small groups rivaled what we had in the '70s, and I agreed to go.

He was right. It was far better than the tavern! The presence of God was strong among us each week when we met, and I realized something important. Everyone wants to be a part of a group of people where they are loved, help others, and find meaning and purpose in life. My friends at the tavern were working hard to create fellowship among themselves, and they did manage to create the human parts of it. They just never discovered a spiritual meaning and purpose for their lives. This explains why many turned to booze instead of Jesus.

Home Fellowship Groups

For years, churches have created home fellowship groups for members to experience a time of being together, to eat a meal, and pray for each other. In addition, the members are asked to help each other out between meetings, if there's time.

For the most part, traditional home fellowship groups achieve all they are designed to do. Millions of Christians gather in homes each week and are doing it right. The problem, however, is that loving one another is the main goal. Within six months, a home fellowship group has achieved its goal and stagnation sets in. There's no challenge the group needs to achieve beyond maintaining what they're doing.

For many years, the church has characterized *fellowship* in this way. This has made for a lot of dissatisfaction, especially when it comes to small group involvement.

It's Time to Redefine "Fellowship"

The word fellowship is a deep word, scripturally speaking. In 1 John 1:3, John gives us a glimpse of the depth of fellowship when he writes, *"We proclaim to you what we have seen and heard, so that you also may have fellowship with us. And our fellowship is with the Father and with His Son, Jesus Christ."* What John is describing is a communion with God the Father and God the Son, Jesus Christ. In verse 7, Paul goes on to share that when Christians have discovered this communion with God, they are also in communion with each other.

When God's people enter into fellowship with Him and each other as described here, there are powerful results. The intertwined relationship with God causes them to be transformed into completely different persons. The relationship also brings physical and emotional healing to their lives. Paul describes it enthusiastically in 2 Corinthians 5:17: *"Therefore, if anyone is in Christ, he is a new creation; the old has gone, the new has come!"*

Paul's understanding of fellowship was exciting. For many Christians, "fellowship" in their minds does not live up to how Paul saw it. To them, it just means getting together with other Christians and eating a meal, which is ok, but not *exciting*.

When a word has lost its definition in a society, other words or terms are used to define the original concept. *Biblical community* is one of those terms. Think of a biblical community as a typical home fellowship group on steroids, without negative side effects. It grows with new members. The exciting life it experiences is so contagious that it attracts others from beyond the four walls of the living room where it meets. It is a place where Christians gather to experience

Christ in their midst. This is the fellowship John describes as the first century church.

That's the kind of small group I want! How about you? Don't you want to be a part of a biblical community that experiences God in such a way that it radically transforms you and those around you? Or, how about experiencing the presence of Christ in such a way that you'll burst if you don't tell someone?

This book is all about helping you to discover ways you and your small group can embrace biblical community. Without a doubt, it will be a challenge to put into practice what I have written here. Nothing good comes easy! The best part about this challenge is that you're not alone. You have God and other Christians from your small group on the journey, all moving in the same direction. How could you lose? All you really have to do is to be willing to take the time to apply what you read.

Making Room for What's Important

Let's do a little mental experiment together. Take a jar and fill it with large rocks, right up to the top. Is the jar full?

Yes and no. It's full of rocks for sure!

Now take some small pebbles and pour a few into the jar to fill in the spaces between the rocks. Add as many as you can. Is the jar full?

Yes and no. It is filled with rocks and pebbles, but there's probably more room for something smaller.

Add sand to the jar to fill in the tiny spaces between the pebbles until you can add no more. Now the jar is truly full, right?

Well, you're almost there. Now pour water into the jar. You won't be able to add much, but the water will absolutely fill that jar completely.

Wait! The experiment isn't over. Remove the rocks, pebbles, sand, and water from the jar and try to fill it back up with the same contents in a different order. What will happen?

If the sand or pebbles are put in first, the rocks won't fit! And so it goes with our priorities in life. We must insure we do the big things first. If we do, the small things fit in fine.

You may be thinking, "I don't really have the time to read this book, let alone spend more time with other people in my small group!" You know, I'm feeling the same way about writing this book. I just don't have the time to write, edit, and get this book to the printer on time. I have a family, a small group that my wife and I co-lead, a full-time job heading up an organization that involves lots of travel, a hobby I enjoy, a golden retriever that needs a bath every two weeks and, well, I could go on and on.

The bottom line is that we all lead very busy lives filled with responsibility. We're pulled in a half-dozen directions at the same time, leaving little to no time to add a handful of new, time-consuming relationships to an already packed schedule!

But, we always find time for what's important, don't we? I found the time to finish this book and get it to the printer. It wasn't a big rock for me, but a very important pebble in my life. Deepening my relationships with my family and home group members is my *larger* priority. In case you're wondering, yes, my dog has been bathed regularly. I guess that would be the water in the experiment we did earlier!

By prioritizing my time on the bigger issues of life, everything fits as it should. And so it will be for you as well when you embrace a lifestyle of biblical community. I don't exactly understand how God does it, but He's always faithful to multiply the time for those who keep living in biblical community at the top of the priority list as a big rock.

The key to making this change in lifestyle is to start small, by implementing one thing at a time.

So, start small right here and right now. Make a decision to finish reading this book!

You're not too busy to learn about how you and your small group can find a powerful, fulfilling, and exciting new way to live, are you? Read a few pages every morning as part of your quiet time with God if you are not a reader. Before you pick up the book to read each morning, ask God to show you a truth that you can share with a family member, a friend, or another small group member each day.

I believe that if you finish reading this book and share what you're learning with others along the way, you'll put much of it into practice without realizing you are doing it. While some things I share here may take a little work, many of my written thoughts are just common sense things you may already be doing, but with a *twist*. You may find that the twist (my way of looking at the activity through a community-based view) makes an event or meeting powerful for building biblical community with fellow small group members.

By living in biblical community with my home group members, I'm getting just as much done as before, but I'm not running on empty all the time. For the most part, my emotional, spiritual, and physical reserves stay full. God has given me a balance in life and a newfound understanding of how the world seems to tug at me in the opposite direction of how God designed me. Wouldn't you enjoy a new level of emotional, spiritual and physical energy in your life? Then get busy reading and apply as much as you can.

Apply it!
- Choosing to live in biblical community is putting God's big priorities in your life before the pebbles or the sand that our world tells us to add first. The choice will keep you balanced and centered on what's most important. If you are not familiar with Matthew 6:25-34, take a few minutes to read this important passage now and meditate on it. Ask God to reveal the "big rocks" He wants you to put in your life's jar first. What pebbles and grains of sand have you put into your jar first that God would challenge you to put in last to make room for more important, everlasting things?

Share it!

- Often, sharing what God is telling you about your priorities is the best way to reinforce the changes you may need to make in your life. At your next small group gathering, share with the group that you are examining your priorities in life to make room for biblical community. Ask them to pray for you! When you begin to discover God's priorities, ask the group to hold you accountable to live them out.

Additional Reading

These two resources are excellent and will help you discover God's priorities for your life:

Ordering Your Private World – Gordon MacDonald
Making Room For Life – Randy Frazee

Chapter 2
The Power of Prayer

When Christ died on that cross, He bore our sin, which separated us from God. When we acknowledge that we have sinned against God and that we accept His forgiveness through Christ's shed blood, we open a communication link to the Creator of the universe, the King of Kings and the Lord of Lords! That, my friend, is a powerful connection indeed! I have grown to love prayer because I am a self-professing power *addict*. Let me explain.

I like cars with powerful engines. The more horsepower it has, the more I want to drive it and experience all it has to offer. I like power tools, too... but not the wimpy, cordless models. I long for the contractor-grade, *monster* hammer drill with the torque converter. If it doesn't dim the house lights when I use it, it's not powerful enough!

I feel the same way about coffee makers, hair dryers, vacuum cleaners, computers... you name it. If it's more powerful and within my reach, I'll try to acquire it because I personally believe that the more power I have at my disposal, the better life will be. Oddly enough, one of the most powerful things I have in a drawer at home has no horsepower or electric plug. This would be my trusty pad of paper that has that sticky stuff on the back.

Years ago, a 3M employee was given the task to develop a new kind of paper glue that was better than what was currently being offered to the public. He worked hard, but only developed glue that just wasn't that sticky! It could hold two pieces of paper together, but not permanently. It was not powerful in the conventional sense of the word.

The glue recipe was shelved, but the employee who invented it found that the glue was useful for keeping his bookmarks in place in his church choir hymnal and off the floor. When he removed the little homemade bookmarks, the hymnal pages did not tear.

He applied it to scraps of paper at the 3M offices and gave them to secretaries, who instantly fell in love with them. You know the rest of the story. Post-it® Notes are an important and a "can't live without 'em" part of our lives today.

I use Post-it® Notes for everything! They've quickly become an indispensable part of my life at home, the office and even small group meetings. These little notes help me keep my thoughts in order and make me look really smart! By strategically placing them on the doors of my home and car, I don't forget important things to take to work or to get done that day. Very powerful indeed... just a different kind of power.

Prayer is powerful in multiple ways. God can heal, bring peace, move people's hearts to do the right thing, and provide us with protection, just to name a few. God will always be the best friend we will ever have because of His power and our ability to communicate with Him through prayer.

Lots of people pray every day and don't see God answering their prayers. Ever wonder why?

1 John 5:14 says *"This is the confidence we have in approaching God: that if we ask anything according to his will, he hears us."* God hears our prayers. We need only to allow Him to reveal His will to us. Here are four examples of prayer that demonstrate how God reveals how He listens when we pray according to His will.

"High-Octane" Prayer

A few years ago, my wife Etna worked as an accounting supervisor at an oil company. One of her employees was pregnant and turned very ill. When she called Etna to give her an update, she reported the doctor's bad news. If an infection within her ovaries did not clear up within 72 hours, he would need to do an operation and she would lose her first trimester baby. After Etna heard this news, she called me and asked me to meet her at this lady's apartment during our lunch break and pray for her.

When we arrived, we let ourselves into her home and found our way to her bedroom because she was too weak to get out of bed. We both prayed for her healing, believing God is the same today as He was in the Bible. To our delight, God released His healing power that very moment and she screamed out, "God's healing me right now. I can feel it!" She described pain shooting through her body, but she just knew it was God's hand at work. I must admit that both Etna and I were surprised. We'd never seen God heal someone right in front of our eyes.

Within a day or so, she went back to the doctor for a checkup and no infection or inflammation was found! Months later, she delivered the baby without a problem, and both mother and child are healthy to this day.

Etna and I pray with people to experience *instant* healing now, expecting God to work miracles. Sometimes He chooses to heal while we're praying, and sometimes He works through doctors and medicine or the healing comes slowly. Other times He does not bring healing in ways we can see, but we keep praying for people, knowing that He indeed is *Jehovah Rapha*, "the God who heals."

Etna's employee had been praying for days by herself for healing. God chose to heal her when two more believers joined her. Why? I think that God wanted to show Etna and me that He wants to work through us powerfully. A private healing would not have provided this experience for us. If you need healing, ask a couple of small group members to pray for you and expect God to heal you! Yes, He's that powerful and He wants all men to know it!

"Boomerang" Prayer

Years ago, I was a leader's assistant in a wonderful home group where every member was loved and accepted. It was a wonderful family-like experience.

Then Phil joined our group. He left home when he was twelve and was forced to make it on his own because his mom walked out on the family and his alcoholic dad beat him. As a survival mechanism, Phil developed a very tough hide to cope with the harsh world around him.

He desperately wanted and needed friends who would become a *healthy* family and love him unconditionally. Phil had just moved to town, transferred by his company to work for a year in a local Houston office.

Phil wasn't from our part of the country and had a strong, unfamiliar accent. At his first home group meeting he said, "I'm very loud and opinionated. I don't really care what others think about my ideas or comments; so get used to it! What you see is what you get." In subsequent meetings, Phil arrived after consuming a six-pack of beer instead of eating a proper meal. Needless to say, the group dynamics changed radically and we lost that "family" feeling. I could not get over how easy it was for one new, abrasive person to mess up a perfectly good small group!

As the weeks went by, Phil would rant and rave now and then during meetings, but mostly he sat there and took it all in quietly. He liked to pray when he was feeling especially guilty about something. He would often blurt out the most honest, gut-wrenching prayers—with an occasional curse word thrown in—during worship or ministry time. Truth be told, his prayers of confession were the most transparent I'd ever heard in public. In a completely different way, his confessions, albeit sporadic, made everyone else in the group feel more uncomfortable. In his own unpolished way, Phil raised the bar for the rest of us without knowing it.

All my group leader and I knew to do was to pray. We'd never encountered a person like Phil and had no idea how to handle him. As the leadership over the group, we agreed to meet every Thursday at 6 a.m. and asked God to soften Phil's heart. We petitioned God to show Phil the roots of his nastiness so we could minister to him.

After just a few weeks of rough home group meetings and social contact with Phil, I got honest with God one morning during prayer. I asked God to move Phil to another small group or better yet, back to his home office before his year in Houston was over. It was selfish, but it was honest, that's for sure!

In His infinite wisdom and grand plan, God did not move Phil back home early. Phil remained in our home group for the balance of the year, angering lots of people along the way. But, after praying for Phil consistently, something happened within me and he was no longer offensive.

The more I prayed for Phil, the more compassion God gave me for him. The weeks I didn't pray for Phil, he got under my skin. The only way I could love and accept him was *through* the love of the Father.

Praying for Phil changed me far more than it changed Phil, which is why I call this kind of powerful communication with God "boomerang" prayer. Often, God puts people or circumstances in our path to shape us through prayer and reliance upon Him. In many cases, the people or circumstances don't change that much, but through prayer, we begin to see things through God's eyes and we change.

Lots of Christians miss out on a powerful work that God wants to do in each of us because we don't press in with prayer when we encounter others who are not like us. Do you have a "Phil" in your group? Don't run off or leave your group! Start praying for him or her and ask God to show you His love for them, replacing your own frustration and judgments.

"Bottom of the Well" Prayer

I am confident that everyone who reads this will be very familiar with this kind of prayer. It usually goes something like, "God, if you just let me get these bills paid and my credit card balances brought down, I swear I'll never go shopping again." Or, "God, if you'd just keep my boss from finding out I didn't turn in those reports on time, I promise to work hard in the future and meet all my deadlines."

You may think these kinds of prayers have no power because it's too easy to fall right back into the same problem. If prayed alone and without accountability, I must agree. When I've employed these "plea bargain prayers" to God, I should have said, "I'm about to make a promise You know I won't keep, but here it goes anyway!"

When Etna and I were dating, I shared with her that I was desperately trying to get out of credit card debt. I owed a little over $2000 and was barely making my minimum payments. With rent, a sports car payment, high auto insurance, and gas to get back and forth to work, I just wasn't making enough to lower my balances with the mounting interest I was paying. I hardly had enough for food, not to mention the high cost of courting a girl in the 1980s!

Etna and I were going to a home group at the time, which is where we met and began to date. I shared this with my group, and Etna was very helpful in inviting me over for dinner many weeknights and provided encouragement when I took a second job. Etna and our small group prayed for me often concerning this issue.

Another good friend in the home group held me accountable to put any extra money toward my debt, and for the next six months, I paid down those credit cards and finally received statements showing a zero balance. Praise the Lord! I never could have done it without their prayer, support, and accountability.

Because I prayed a "bottom of the well" prayer in the company of other believers, and was willing to submit myself to them and be accountable for a change in direction—the true meaning of "repentance"—I got out and more importantly *stayed out* of credit card debt to this day.

God honors everyone who cries out to Him for help as long as He knows they will be good stewards of what He gives. In most cases, stewardship includes submitting to the accountability of others who love you and know what is right. If you thought "bottom of the well" prayers were never answered, think again. If you're willing to confess the sin, repay the debt or make things right, and be held accountable to change directions and live as God would have you live, He will answer your prayer with a yes!

"I love you" Prayer

When I was a kid, my dad traveled a great deal as part of his work. When he came home from a trip, the whole family was happy to have him home. But, like most little boys, I saw this reunion as far more than having my dad back at home. He always brought me a little gift that I was eager to receive. After a few of his trips overseas where the little gifts were especially interesting, I remember greeting him with "What did you bring me?" instead of "Daddy, I'm glad you're home." My older brother told me how selfish that attitude was and that I should not ask about gifts upon his arrival in the future. It was quite hard, but I could see he appreciated being loved for who he was, not the gifts he brought.

For years, I approached God that same way. The "gimmie" attitude was my only daily interaction with the Lord! This distorted my understanding of God and kept me from seeing what He'd already provided without request.

Today I pray differently, which has changed the way I view God and life. Each day, I thank God for another day in which to partner with Him in building the kingdom. I thank Him for all the ways He protects me that I *don't* see. I thank Him in advance for making a way where there seems to be no solution when I am confident it will increase the kingdom of God.

Because of God's indescribable love for each of us, I do not think He dislikes our constant requests for salvation from disease, illness, financial burden, or relationship problems. But, the psalmist David modeled something important for us, which is to simply come before God and praise Him for who He is, not what He can do for us in our moment of need. One of the many praises David offered to the Lord is found in Psalm 34. The entire Psalm is an excellent example of praising God without request. Here are the first ten verses so you can see the difference between a praise and a request:

> *I will extol the Lord at all times; his praise will always be on my lips.*
> *My soul will boast in the Lord; let the afflicted hear and rejoice.*
> *Glorify the Lord with me; let us exalt his name together.*
>
> *I sought the Lord, and he answered me; he delivered me from all my fears.*
> *Those who look to him are radiant; their faces are never covered with shame.*

This poor man called, and the Lord heard him;
he saved him out of all his troubles.
The angel of the Lord encamps around those
who fear him, and he delivers them.

Taste and see that the Lord is good; blessed is the
man who takes refuge in him.
Fear the Lord, you his saints, for those who fear
him lack nothing.
The lions may grow weak and hungry, but those
who seek the Lord lack no good thing.

When you make a regular habit of entering into God's presence for the purpose of praise and adoration for who He is—with no personal agenda or laundry list of stuff you want Him to do—you will begin to understand the numerous ways He has already provided for you. This shapes the way you make future requests, and helps you keep your priorities in line with building the kingdom of God instead of the kingdoms of this world.

When you next meet with the Lord for a time of prayer, spend some time praising Him! Between worship songs in upcoming small group meetings, boldly proclaim how wonderful God is the way David did throughout the Psalms. I think you'll find that you can take your level of worship to a whole new level with this kind of prayer.

The Common Thread

There is a common thread running through each of these four types of prayers I've illustrated here. This thread brings these widely different kinds of prayer directly into our ongoing discovery of what it means to live in biblical community and what makes it so powerful.

Prayer provides protection when we pray with others. Ecclesiastes 4:12 states, *"Though one may be over-powered, two can defend themselves. A cord of three strands is not quickly broken."* For years, I thought this only applied to married people because I grew up hearing it at weddings. But, it also applies to those who choose to live in community with each other and the Creator.

Scripture refers to Satan as a thief and a lion, roaming the earth to find those whom he can devour. Does this frighten you? The reason this doesn't scare me is because I choose to live in the safest place on earth...in biblical community with those who know me intimately and are willing to stand up for me and watch my back. Praying with my home group members creates a protective shield that Satan cannot penetrate easily.

Prayer becomes powerful when you reach the end of yourself and you don't care who knows you're desperate. When I get to the end of my rope, or choose not to climb my own rope in the first place, I'm telling God, "I have no true control over this illness, situation, or relationship. I give it to You." It is in this place where I begin to live in community with my Creator. It is here that I learn what I must allow Him to do through me and for me. I've found that it has a depth of power all its own when I pray this way aloud and in the witness of others. All who hear the transparent cry for help will also sense their own helplessness or sense of independence that needs to be confessed.

Prayer is powerful when others are praying, too. In Matthew 18:19-20, Jesus states that if two believers agree on earth concerning God's will, it will be done. Moreover, Jesus said that where two or three are gathered in His name, He will be there also. When we pray with other believers, petitioning God to do His will, we enter into a supernatural form of community that ties us together with Christ. That's one powerful and heavenly team!

A Solid Foundation

Last year, Etna and I had our old, dilapidated

garage torn down and a new one built. One morning we went to the office and when we came home, our back fence was removed and our old garage was gone. We were shocked as to how fast it was demolished! Tearing down is a lot easier than building something new and doing it right.

The rest of the project took far longer. The

single greatest element in the whole project was the concrete slab for the new structure. With all the soil samples, inspections and prep work, plus delays because of foul weather, it took nearly three weeks to pour the cement.

When I asked our contractor what was taking so long with the foundation work, he said something that can be directly applied to our discussion about the importance of prayer. He commented, "The foundation is the most important part of this building. If I don't take time to get this right, you'll be demolishing this new garage in no time. I only build garages that last a lifetime, and I do it with an excellent team of guys who know my standards. That's why I was knee deep in dirt when you came home tonight."

This, my friend, is what our Lord, the "Senior Contractor" on the job site, is asking of us! When we begin to build a community based on prayer, we learn how our small group can build the kingdom of God in partnership with Him. Trying to create a powerful small group without prayer is just like building your house upon the sand. It may look good for a while, but when the first storm comes, it will fall like a house of cards.

The Place of Prayer in Community

Prayer takes place on at least three levels in biblical community. Moreover, praying on each level is vital to getting the most out of your small group; so don't cheat yourself by omitting one!

Intimate, Private Prayer

When Etna and I first fell in love, we could not communicate enough. Often, she would call me on the telephone first thing in the morning to wake me and tell me she loved me. What a great way to start the day! Your daily time with God is much the same, and it's an opportunity to tell Him you love Him and receive His unconditional love, which you'll surely need in the hours to come as you inter- act with your family, co-workers, and the world.

Your daily time with God should be relaxed, and it should not be something you feel forced to do, but something you desire. God wants to devel- op a very deep friendship with you, and it becomes deeper with frequency. The more you pray, the more you'll begin to hear His voice—and when you pray, know that God *always* hears you and answers! Just remember that He sometimes answers prayers with "wait" and "no," two answers we don't like to hear.

How familiar and friendly should we become with God, our Creator? Here's an example. A few years ago, a pastor from Idaho kept calling my offices to ask questions about his home groups and how to help them experience true biblical community. We quickly became telephone friends and usually ended our conversations with prayer for one another.

I'll never forget how he prayed for me the first time. He said, "Howdy God! It's me again. Randall and I have just had the best conversation about how to build Your kingdom, and I'm so happy I have made this friend. Would you bless his socks off right now and give him a big, God-sized hug so he knows how much You love him? Thanks, and I'll talk to you later. Amen!"

I could not contain my laughter as he prayed. I'd never heard anyone pray like that, especially a senior pastor! But, he had a special friendship with his Creator, and I wanted that same kind of familiarity with God. It wasn't flippant either—when this pastor prayed, it was reverent, but not stuffy or formal.

In the days to follow, I began to practice praying this way in my daily time with God, and it revolutionized my daily "quiet time" and made it anything but quiet! God and I began to have ongoing conversations about anything and everything while I sat in traffic, mowed the lawn, washed my hair in the shower, and even dreamed at night. Amazing! Praying alone each day shapes our hearts and gives us God's vision for others and the many decisions we need to make. There's simply no way we can experience God's purpose for our life without it.

Praying with your Earthly Family

Years ago when I was first married, I found that the less Etna and I prayed together, the more we disagreed on various issues—and at times, those disagreements turned into heated arguments!

If you are married, pray with your wife or husband every single day. Don't waste the time to complain to God about them, or pick a fight during your time of prayer. Thank God for them, ask Him to pour out His love and wisdom on them, and protect his or her mind from the enemy! Pray about the tasks or issues of the day, and claim God's promises for one another.

Satan can easily drive a wedge between you and your spouse if you don't pray together daily. I've spent countless hours with small group members whose marriages were on the rocks, and in every single case, they have reported that they rarely prayed with one another each day.

If you have children, pray with them every day as well. Often, parents pray with their children before they go to sleep at night. This is one of my most cherished memories as a child! My mother tucked me in and we would pray together. But, as I look back on my days growing up in my household, the prayer time that my whole family enjoyed around the breakfast table was equally as important and far more powerful. It was in those early morning moments that we banded together as one to lift up requests on behalf of other family members. This kept our family strong and kept Satan from gaining a foothold in our relationships.

A long time ago, I saw a refrigerator magnet that had this phrase inscribed on it: "The family that prays together stays together." I always thought that rhyme was a little cheesy, but judging from the millions of families who have been broken apart by divorce, I'd have to say that praying with your spouse and children is probably the greatest single thing you can do to protect your family.

Praying as a Small Group—Your Spiritual Family
Your spiritual family is comprised of other

Christians with whom you regularly interact. This usually includes some of your earthly family members and close friends who know Jesus and live near enough to enjoy one another's company. While your church as a whole is indeed a spiritual family, it's a much larger group that probably does not provide the sense of intimacy to which I am referring here.

I consider my small group my spiritual family and you should too. I pray for my fellow group members as often as possible. Each morning as I drive to work I pray for their relationships, personal needs, and that God will use them mightily that day to be "salt and light" to the world around them.

Praying for my fellow group members every day also conditions my heart. The more I pray, the more I see how God views them. This becomes vitally important when we disagree or find ourselves in conflict.

Prayer Ideas:

The "Prayer Call" at Work
One of my favorite ways to encourage another group member is to call them at work and pray for

them. I always ask if they have a few minutes to talk, then I ask how their day or week is going. Usually, they'll tell me about a project that they're working on or one they've just finished. Sometimes, they'll quietly tell me they've had a run in with a co-worker or boss and that it's tense around the office. I use whatever they share with me as a reason to pray for them on the phone. I praise God for a completed project, ask Him to give them stamina and a clear mind for the task at hand, or peace about a situation that is beyond my friend's control. The call usually doesn't take more than five minutes unless we're both off the clock. Usually I'm told, "Wow! I can't believe you'd call me at the office just to pray for me. Thanks!"

The "Prayer Visit" in a Home

Another great way to pray with fellow small group members is to make a prayer visit into their home. I schedule this after the dinner hour. If the family has children, I ask if we can come over for 15 minutes and pray with the parents after the children have gone to sleep. If I know the parents are having problems with discipline in the house, or if a child is ill, I will ask if we can come over near the bedtime hour and pray with the child as well. When we arrive, we usually refuse offers of food or drinks because we've invited ourselves into their home and we don't want to be there too long. We usually gather in the living room, and I ask them if there are any specific things going on in the household about which we can pray. If they have nothing to share, or have a lot to share but don't feel ready to share it, I simply pray a blessing over the home, each person by name, and their relationships with family, co-workers, bosses, and neighbors. When your small group leader or pastor comes to your home to pray for you and your family, receive God's power and word through them. You will be blessed. If your small group leader invites you to go along to pray for someone, jump at the opportunity! You will see God move through you in a special way. Moreover, you will grow in your ministry to others. If you know of someone who needs this kind of prayer, talk with your small group leader and make a plan for how best to bless this person. It's a very powerful way to invest 15 minutes into another member or family in your group.

The "Prayer Walk"

Everyone needs to get some exercise and we all need to pray more. Why not combine the two? Ask a fellow small group member if you can meet them outside their front door for a morning walk. Instead of talking about prayer requests, just begin to voice them aloud as you walk. As you pass each home in the neighborhood, ask God for peace for each household and favor with them. Petition God for the kind of friendships with them that will help them see His love through you and the other members of the small group. So you'll know, this kind of prayer is one of the best preparations you can make for a small group-sponsored neighborhood barbeque, which we'll discuss in depth in another chapter.

As you incorporate these kinds of prayer into your lifestyle, never forget that prayer is a form of spiritual warfare. There are dark forces that become powerless when we boldly approach the throne of God because of what Christ did for us on the cross. The more we pray alone and with others from our group, the harder it will be for Satan to worm his way into our minds and relationships!

Apply it!

- Praying with others in your group will come naturally for some, but frankly, our world is busy and we often just make enough time to pray for ourselves or not at all. So, to create a new habit, you'll have to schedule your daily prayer times and prayer visits on a calendar. After a month or so, it will become a natural part of life. When you see the results, you'll never want to stop.

- Journaling is also a great way to record your prayers and thoughts as you pray. As I look back at the things I've written, I am always amazed at how God has answered prayer and met needs.

- Find a time and place where you will go and pray each day. Bring your journal and your Bible with you. Just sit silently and wait on God for a few minutes. There's no rush! Then, thank Him for who He is and how He has blessed you. Or, find a Psalm to read to Him aloud. Next, begin to pray for each member of your group by name as well as your family and friends. When you pray for unchurched friends, pray for yourself as much as you pray for them—asking God to give you His love for them and His words to share.

Share it!

I hope this chapter on prayer has motivated you to pray more. If so, tell your small group that you're going to pray more and invite them to join you. Praying with others is a great way to help them discover a heart for God and unchurched people, too.

Additional Reading
An Appointment with the King – Joel Comiskey

Chapter 3
Lean On Me

In 1972, Bill Withers released a song that was number one on the charts for many weeks. While you may not remember his name, if you're over 40 you probably know the tune. The words to the song could not better describe what small group members should be for one another:

Sometimes in our lives we all have pain
We all have sorrow
But if we are wise
We know that there's always tomorrow

Lean on me, when you're not strong
And I'll be your friend
I'll help you carry on
For it won't be long
'Til I'm gonna need
Somebody to lean on

Please swallow your pride
If I have things you need to borrow
For no one can fill those of your needs

That you don't let show
If there is a load you have to bear
That you can't carry
I'm right up the road
I'll share your load
If you just call me

So just call on me brother, when you need a
hand. We all need somebody to lean on.
I just might have a problem that you'd
understand. We all need somebody to lean on.

This song touches on many important aspects of healthy small group life such as deep friendship, transparency, serving others, and allowing others to serve us. When we consider others more important than ourselves, it brings both balance and perspective to our lives. It's nearly impossible to be self-centered when we're serving out of pure motives. There's also one more benefit. When we help carry the burdens of others, we begin to view our own burdens in a far different way.

As you continue to read this chapter, let the lyrics—and the tune, if you're old enough to remember—get into your heart and move you to see the other members of your group in a new way.

Turning Members into Connected Friends

At forty-two years of age, I have a handful of true, life-long friends. There's John, my best friend from high school who kept me out of all sorts of trouble as a young man. Then there's Joe and Scott, college buddies who prayed for me often and loved me unconditionally during the most difficult years of my life thus far. But, I don't get to spend much time with them today. Sure, we talk on the phone occasionally and promise to call more, but we all live in different places and have families of our own. We're just too busy with life now to call each other "connected" friends.

I also have a group of people with whom I have made a conscious decision to include in my life as much as possible. This well-connected group of friends is my small group!

The relationships I've made in my small group are quite deep. Why? We work hard to help each other grow spiritually, and this requires us to pray for one another often, spend time together, and urge each other to do God's will. The relationships are also powerful because our daily interaction with one another increases the kingdom of God and diminishes the kingdoms of this world. If this doesn't make sense yet, just keep reading and you'll see what I'm talking about.

The "Two-Hour Meeting" versus the "Six Days and Twenty-two Hours In Between"

For many, being a member of a small group is a commitment to show up at group meetings each week. While this is certainly important—and we'll discuss what makes small group meetings great in a later chapter—the time *between* meetings is just as important.

In a typical week, I'll spend a couple of hours on the phone with other group members and an additional number of hours with one member or another in face-to-face interaction. When we talk on the phone, I usually have nothing in particular I need from them. I'm just calling to see how their week is going, how I can be praying for them, and just as importantly, when they might have time to spend with me. Why? That's what friends do! They call each other just to chat and work hard to find the time to be together, even if it's just to eat a slice of pizza and watch a movie on Saturday night. How does this look in action?

Be Casual and Laid Back

Last night Russell came over to my house around 8 p.m., and we went to Starbucks for a cup of coffee. We sat outside and talked for an hour or so, and then we came back to the house so I could get a few things done before work the next day. It wasn't a whole evening together, but it was very valuable for both of us. We talked about our relationships and spiritual matters as well, agreeing to pray for one another in areas where we need God to break through or give us wisdom.

As we were finishing our coffee, I asked Russell to give me some input on what kind of tires I should buy for my car. After all, we're guys and there's time for personal talk and then there's time to get serious and talk about cars!

Through these regular times of talking and praying together, Russell and I are becoming great friends. I've been where he is in life, so I know from experience how to pray for him. Russell knows more about cars and he's always happy to share what he knows. While we don't give one another a lot of advice, we do pray for each other and with each other as well. After all, prayer is far more powerful than advice.

Have Fun!

Years ago, Etna regularly picked up a friend down the street and met a couple of other women from our small group at the Farmer's Market a couple of miles from home. It was a fun time for all of them, and they consistently found treasures at garage sales on the way home.

In our last small group, we had a single, college-aged guy who always showed up to church and small group meetings in wrinkled clothes. Etna invited him over for dinner and told him to bring his dirty laundry. We ate dinner while the first load was washing and drying. After dinner, he helped us wash dishes and clean the kitchen. Then, Etna showed him how to hang up clothes as soon as they were dry to eliminate the wrinkles and prevent the need for ironing. Seems mundane, but that's what this guy needed most: a mother figure who would feed him and help him learn how to look presentable. Oddly enough, his mother called a few months later after he'd gone back to finish his senior year of college at Purdue and thanked Etna for picking up where she'd left off with her cooking and laundry lessons.

Ask for Help

A number of weeks ago, I had an evening flight home that was delayed due to rain. I finally arrived bleary-eyed at 1 a.m. Remember Russell? I called him from out of town and asked him to pick me up, even though it was the middle of the night. Could Etna have picked me up? Sure! But asking Russell to do this was far more powerful for our friendship because close friends ask each other for sacrificial favors. I wanted Russell to know I considered him a close friend.

I hope you see a pattern of relational involvement developing with these stories. Etna and I *invent* ways to spend time with the people in our group and look for ways to get involved in their lives. We do this because God has put us together for a special reason, and we want to be successful in whatever God has in store for us. We also know that the more we love one another in our small group by investing time into each other's lives, the less Satan will be able to divide us when it comes time to work as a team.

In every group in which I've been a member, I have developed wonderful friendships. Take time to become friends with the other people in your small group outside that two-hour period during the week when your group formally meets. You'll find that by spending time with them on projects like yard work or car repair, going shopping, or just watching a movie, they're on your mind during your quiet times with God.

A time investment prompts you to pray for them. When you're with them next, you'll be given grace and a new understanding of God's love for them. It's by far the most powerful part of community I've ever experienced. I've seen God move mountains in people's lives, minds, and bodies because I took the time to befriend, serve, and pray for them.

The Stages of Maturity in Small Group Life

As you work hard to become good friends with the other members of your small group, it's only fair to tell you that groups go through stages of maturity. Here's a brief description of each one:

The Forming Stage – When your group first forms, the members will probably know one another's names, what each one does for a living, and how many kids they have, but that's about it. It's a lot like a newlywed couple on their honeymoon. A commitment to a relationship has been made, but the people don't really understand to whom they are committing!

In the first few weeks of a new small group's formation, don't expect a great deal of deep, transparent sharing. Opinions of others are still being formed. The members of your group don't know if they can trust the other small group members with deep issues or heavy prayer requests. Just enjoy the first few weeks together and make an effort to get to know various members of your group. Ask a lot of questions and share as much as you feel comfortable sharing.

Just a few months ago, Etna and I started a new group. While our members bonded quickly, we helped the process along by inviting various people from our group over for dinner. We even took a meeting night off to play miniature golf together.

This first stage usually lasts about two months, but can be longer or shorter depending on the makeup of the group. The key to moving through this stage is to get to know others and let them get to know you.

The Storming Stage – As indicated by its name, it's clear that your small group's honeymoon is over. It's been a month or two, and your small group members now know enough about each other to find something to dislike! This is normal and an important part of small group life and maturity.

I recall a group where one of my fellow members would pray for what seemed like an eternity, consuming most of the time we had to pray as a group. It infuriated me because he seemed incredibly selfish and oblivious to others. He also added to the problem by saying "Lord" repeatedly while he prayed. One night, I counted over 200 "Lords" in five minutes! Every time he prayed, I wanted to walk over to him whack him on the arm and say, "I think your

record has a scratch in it and your needle is stuck!"

I became so sour toward him that I didn't even want to go to our meetings if I knew he was going to be there. Our group leader didn't seem to find it annoying, but I knew others in the group were bothered by it as well. Out of sheer boredom, I would look around the room when he prayed his long, verbose prayers. Often, I'd make eye contact with others in the group who didn't have their eyes closed and heads bowed. I'm not sure if they saw my expression, but numerous times I caught their wide-eyed looks that said, "Will *someone* shut this guy down so we can get on with our meeting?"

A few weeks later, our group leader was on vacation and he asked me to facilitate the ministry time that night. I thought it would be a good time to talk about prayer and my leader said it was fine as long as my heart was in the right place before bringing it up. So that night, I asked this man if he felt strongly about any aspect of prayer while we were gathered as a group.

To my surprise and delight, he said, "I don't think anyone should pray too long when we're in a meeting like this. I know I'm the worst on this issue, and I really need everyone's help. If I go on and on like I have done in the past, someone should just tap me on the knee or shoulder and I'll wrap it up quickly! I really love to pray and always lose myself in prayer when I get started."

When I heard this, God instantly gave me a

new understanding of how much this man loved Jesus! While he never stopped the repetitive use of the word "Lord", I didn't seem to be bothered by it any longer. The fact that we discussed it openly and he acknowledged he was doing it and needed help made all the difference in the world. The discussion softened my heart and actually turned anger into admiration. This man had an amazing prayer life and mine was minimal at the time.

Conflict in your small group can arise out of anything and everything. Opinions about spiritual gifts, strongly-held beliefs about God or the Bible, home schooling versus public or private schooling, political affiliation, race, how much money some members make compared to others, are all issues that small group members can have with one another.

Every group goes through a period of conflict they must work through, and the common ground is usually agreeing to a third idea or answer about something. Settling other issues just comes down to "agreeing to disagree" by embracing the diversity of backgrounds and opinions.

The key to working through conflict in your small group is to keep the lines of communication open. Also, developing friendships outside the meeting and praying fervently for each member everyday will help you and your group move past this stage and continue to grow together. The conflict stage is all about learning how to find and embrace God's love for one another. Without God's love, it's a recipe for lots of hurt feelings, arguments, and a group that never achieves biblical community.

It's unfortunate that some small groups never get beyond the conflict stage. At the first sign of discord, members put up their defenses or leave the group assuming that Christians are not supposed to have conflict. This could not be further from the truth. Christians are ordinary humans who are devoted to following an extraordinary God.

All small groups go through some conflict between members or what might be termed growing pains. It may not be a huge blow up, but there is always a little friction between people as they get to know one another and learn to love each other, warts and all.

The Norming Stage – As your group resolves conflict, you will find yourself in a wonderful time in small group life. This stage is characterized by a respect for others despite differences of opinion.

When a group has normed, idiosyncrasies are over-looked and even humored. Your group is becoming a healthy spiritual family that does not let conflict dissuade you or break you apart.

When your group moves into this stage of maturity, enjoy it! Hang out with each other between meetings, do fun things together, and spend time together praying. But don't get comfortable. This stage is not the last stage or should never be the goal of your group or it will stagnate.

Etna and I were part of a young married couples' group that was absolutely the best group we've ever been in. We had all been married a year or two and didn't have kids yet. We were constantly over at one another's homes for dinner and to hang out on weekends. The group quickly became our spiritual family.

The problem with this group was that no one thought about inviting others to join us and enjoy what we'd found together. If new young married couples showed up at our church, they were invited to join us, but as a whole, we didn't go looking for them. We'd achieved everything we wanted to achieve in the group, and now it was just a matter of maintaining our intimacy.

It wasn't long before this group began to lose

members. Some left our group and stayed in the church, while others moved on to different churches. Why? We had achieved our goal of being a close-knit group of Christians and it was time to move on.

As I reflect on this wonderful small group of friends we enjoyed for a year or so, I can see our group placed the finish line of our race somewhere in the middle of the course. The Designer of our race, however, wanted us to run further and cross the *real* finish line!

God gives us a wonderful sense of fellowship and community with other believers for a couple of important reasons. In community, there is safety in numbers. Satan has a far harder time tempting us to sin and do our own thing when we have Christian brothers and sisters around us praying for and encouraging us. God has also given us a strong sense of family unity to help others find what we now enjoy as believers.

Winning the race in small group life is not just becoming a spiritual family for fun and protection from Satan. It's to do something powerful with God, which is what we'll discuss in the last stage of small group life.

The Performing Stage – If you thought the norming stage was the bomb, you ain't seen nothin' yet! This is where small group life goes from great to incredible. Unlike groups who focus on norming as the goal, it won't fizzle out if you move on to this stage of maturity.

In the mid '90s, I was leading a small group who had just entered into the norming stage and we really loved one another. The members also had very strong prayer lives and had a strong sense we were to invite others who were unchurched to join us.

We spent time praying for people we knew at work, near our homes, and friends we'd made throughout our lives. To keep track of everyone we were praying for, we used a large poster with their first names on it and taped it to the wall for our meetings.

Between meetings, we met one another's co-workers by going to lunch during the week as our schedules allowed. We also strategically had our friends over for dinner and invited small group members to join us so they could get to know each other. It was as if our unchurched friends were bugs, drawn to a light at night! They liked what they saw—genuine friendships and a newfound understanding of God's love among people.

When we felt new friendships had formed between members and member's friends, we invited them to come to Sunday services with us or to a weekly small group meeting. A number of them visited, and most of them joined our group!

It was really quite exciting to see people come into a new understanding of God. One young woman would come to small group meetings and say, "I found the coolest scripture about how God protects us from our enemies. My new enemy is fear, and with God I know I won't be scared any more."

This, my friend, is transformation. People being transformed into new creatures in Christ happens naturally when a maturing spiritual family like your small group reaches out to those who will see God through you!

The transformation does not end with the new people coming into your small group. God will begin to transform you as well by giving you the opportunity to be a big brother or sister to the "newbies" in your group.

The performing stage is all about extending God's love to those who don't yet know it and harnessing the love a small group has gained through the previous stages of maturity. This will give your group a sense of purpose beyond yourselves. If your groups experience anything like mine did, you'll have such a deep love for one another that you'll think what you had in the norming stage was just puppy love. God just loves to bless people who are about His business.

Remember this about the stages of small group life. As new people come into your small group, you will move through the stages again. However, it doesn't take as long to move through the forming and storming stages when new members come into an established group, so don't be too concerned. When new folks are invited in, your group will have enough momentum to absorb any personality conflicts that may arise.

Tips for Success

To move through these stages of healthy small group life, you need to adopt the other members of your group as true friends. What characterizes a true friend? A friend is one who can drop by your house without an invitation, grab a soda out of the fridge without asking permission, and flop on your couch with you on a lazy Saturday afternoon when time permits. To enjoy all God has for you in the performing stage, it will require you to make the other members of your group a priority in life, but the results are well worth it.

I can't tell you how much I enjoy my life because of the deep, purpose-filled relationships I've formed in my small group! The other members of my small group know they are always welcome at my home, just as I am welcome in their homes. If it's mealtime, they eat with us. If I'm doing yard-work, I hand them a rake or a weed eater. Or, I'll drop by their house just to visit for a few minutes if I'm in the area.

I know this lifestyle may sound lofty or unat-tainable in our busy society, but if I can do it living in the fourth largest city in the U.S., you can too! Call a fellow small group member with no requests, just to see how they are doing. Invite them to come over and help you with a project, fold laundry, or watch a movie with your family one night. Ask them what projects they are working on around the house and see if you can help out for an hour or two. By doing this, you will find that God will give you a newfound love for them. You'll need this for your goal in small group life, which is not only to enter into biblical community, but extend it to those who have never experienced it.

To keep me on this path, I've made some

lifestyle changes that make all the difference to my personal walk with God and my group's success. I allow others to hold me accountable to grow, and I've rekindled a passion to spend time with others, despite my hectic schedule.

Accountability

Because I want to keep growing in my spiritual walk with God, I meet with another guy in my group and we ask each other hard questions. It's difficult to describe how valuable mutual accountability is for me, but I'll try. By sharing the weakest areas of my character with someone from my small group who loves me deeply, I feel as if I can conquer the world despite my flaws. I'm loved regardless! The weekly small group meetings also help me to say no to temptation when it comes, and believe me, temptation lurks around every corner in my life!

What kinds of things do we discuss? Anything and everything. Finances and debt, attitudes, how much attention we give our wives, our time usage, our relationships (with family, co-workers, and persons of the opposite sex), our ever-straying thought life, the websites we've visited since we last met, etc. Come to think of it, there's really nothing that's "off limits." Our level of transparency has grown as we continue to disclose things about ourselves and become increasingly vulnerable.

Have I ever held something back? Yes. I have told my accountability partner that I have something I know I need to share but I'm just not ready to do it. He's always been supportive and patient with me and I try to be the same with him.

Eventually, I do share everything that is bugging me about myself or that I know I can't conquer alone. The reason I can be this transparent is because I know that what is shared there will stay there. We have agreed never to talk about the other's issues outside of our time together. If we feel we need to tell our wives so we can pray into the situation, we ask for permission first.

If you're not in an accountable relationship with another guy or gal from your small group, ask your small group leader to help you find one! Get together with this person each week for coffee or to walk around a park and just begin by talking to them about whatever you feel comfortable sharing. Let the relationship deepen naturally and continue to offer more of yourself as you ask your partner about deeper issues.

I'd like to give you one strong pointer though. Don't offer advice until you've prayed about it long and hard and know it's what God wants you to say. Most people don't want advice from a friend nearly as often as they just want someone to listen and hear their heart.

When you form this kind of accountable relationship with someone in your small group, you'll find it will give you a comfort level in group meetings you have not experienced before. It will also help you to see that no one is perfect and everyone has issues they need to work through.

We just can't go through life with lots of deep hurts and hidden secrets without it taking a huge toll on our spiritual and emotional well-being. Accountability helps us discover, work through, and find freedom from issues that keep us from enjoying God's purposes in our lives.

The Value of "Wasting Time"

Years ago, I bought my first day planner. Within a month, it became as important to me as my Bible. I referred to it once an hour or more throughout the day and evening, scheduling my time to get far more accomplished than ever before. I was meeting with different people and keeping track of all kinds of things on my lists and getting things done. What an innovation!

However, one "to do" never appeared on my calendar pages. I never wrote down "sit around and do nothing with a friend." Why? That would be a complete waste of time!

If it were not for a pastor in my church who was mentoring me at the time, I would have worked myself into an early grave. He sat me down, looked at my day planner, and told me that I had forgotten to schedule enough time for what's really important—relating to others to maintain balance in my life.

It took a number of years for me to come to grips with what he challenged me to do. I just couldn't make radical changes in my lifestyle and values overnight. Some of it stemmed from being in debt and having to make enough money to keep up payments to credit card companies. The balance was due to the society in which we live and how I was raised. Both my parents were incredibly busy with work and church activities throughout my childhood. In my mind, productivity had always translated into marking some objective off a list somewhere. If I didn't pay a bill or get a list of tasks accomplished, it wasn't a good day.

Today I've discovered why God commanded us to take a sabbath. Rest has great productive value and is by no means a waste of time. God commanded us to take a day of rest for our own sanity! When we prioritize relaxing at home with our friends and family, it provides an emotional, mental, physical, and spiritual balance we need to survive and remain in balance.

Each week, I schedule at least one evening where Etna and I spend time with other small group members or friends. Some weeks, our friends are busy, so we invest that evening relaxing or calling someone to talk for no reason in particular.

On either Saturday or Sunday each week, I try to avoid lots of activities and snooze on the couch for an hour or two.

This may seem like the life of leisure and completely unattainable for you, but it can be done if it's a priority. After all, we always find time for what's important. Let me encourage you to plan times like this in your busy schedule if it does not happen naturally. Don't let circumstances control you. It may take months or even a year to work a free night and a free Saturday or Sunday into your life, but do what it takes to make room for life!

Most people are too busy because they've become a slave to one or more things in this world. It could be the number of activities in which you've enrolled your children or the inability to say the word "no."

To get the most out of your small group, you'll need to invest some energy each week into "wasting time" with your family and others in your group. If you feel guilty and need permission to do this, I heartily grant you permission right here and now. It's your calendar! Take your time by the reins and decide who's in control! Refuse to be a "time victim" any longer.

I had the opportunity to apply this last week when my friend Ron called me at work to ask if we had plans for the evening. Ron comes to our small group as often as he can make it. My mind raced with all the things I *should* be working on, such as writing this book, searching the internet for car parts I need, or cleaning my fish tank. All three were important things I wanted to get done in the next few days. But, I realized that I had not taken a break to relax in a number of days, so I asked him what he had in mind.

As I suspected, Ron wanted to know if Etna and I would be interested in playing an addictive board game we'd played together in the past. I made a quick call to Etna, who liked the idea. Ron came over that night, and we invited our mutual friend, Cynthia, to join us so we'd have a foursome.

Let's see… what did we accomplish? That night, Ron shared that he'd been to the doctor and found out he had a medical concern that needed prayer. I mentioned that I needed to clean my fish tank and Cynthia said she wanted to watch me, and Ron watched too. So, I took fifteen minutes between games to clean the glass and feed the fish. I'm not sure why she wanted to see me scrape green stuff off the glass, but anytime someone has an interest in my aquarium it makes me happy.

That night, everyone had a good laugh when the team who was dreadfully behind in the first round of the board game won the second one quickly. Before the evening was over, we discovered that another friend's birthday was coming up and we discussed ways we could make it extra-special for them.

What appeared to be "wasted time" turned into a very productive evening, even though I had not written it in my day planner. A person shared a prayer need without pressure to do so. There were a couple of times that night when we all laughed, which is very important to maintaining balance in life for me. I also inadvertently taught Cynthia how to take care of my fish when we went on vacation. Wasting time together with others is never really a waste of time. This is where we discover how we can love one another.

While it may not seem as if you're accomplishing anything or being productive when you hang out with other small group members, something valuable is happening indeed. You have chosen to make these people a priority in your life and give them access to your heart issues through open sharing and a life exchange.

As your small group becomes a spiritual family,

expect to become frustrated with certain members. Earlier in this chapter, I shared that conflict is normal and a sign of growth, not gloom and doom for the group. Just remember to pray hard concerning your own attitudes and the words you speak during this time. Look for God's solution to the issues, not man's wisdom or advice.

Satan hates it when Christians spend time together as friends who truly care about one another and are willing to share their lives with friends and family outside the church. His authority is being destroyed and his kingdom is shrinking as the kingdom of God grows. So, for no other reason, investing in other small group members will protect you from the schemes of the devil. You know, his methods haven't changed throughout the centuries. It's always been his strategy to divide and conquer. Living in daily community with the other members of your group and learning to love them as true friends makes him work very hard with few results.

When you're spending time with other believers in your small group to build one another up or serve one another, remember Jesus is there. When fellow small group members come over to your house to eat dinner or watch a movie, Jesus is with you. Christian community is indeed powerful, but to experience the "Christ among us" and the Christ who dwells within others, we must spend time together as true friends!

Apply it!
- Remember the lyrics to the song by Bill Withers? Who in your group would say, "I know I can lean on you because you're there for me"? Take time each day to ask the Lord to reveal how important it is to have friends and to be a true friend to others in your group.
- Schedule some time this next week to invite a small group member to your home to hang out and "waste time" together on a non-small group meeting night.
- Take a break one day this week during business hours and call someone in your small group to find out how they're doing and how you can be praying for them.

Share it!
- Ask your small group leader to help you establish a connection with a person of the same sex from

your small group for accountability. Set up a three month trial partnership, using a goal you need to accomplish or be held accountable to do as the basis for your time together. If the relationship works, renew the partnership and begin to share deeper issues as you both feel led. If it doesn't work out, talk to your partner and figure out what needs to change within you or the other person to make the partnership work.

• When small group members come over to your house, tell them to make themselves at home. Show them where the soft drinks are in the fridge, how to load the dishwasher when they're done with a dish, etc. Begin to treat them like family!

Additional Reading
Refrigerator Rights – Will Miller and Glenn Sparks

Chapter 4
Widening Your Circle

Last year, I was asked by a pastor to visit a small group of dedicated Christians from his church. They had been in a small group together for two years. I showed up about fifteen minutes before the group's official starting time and met a couple of the members around the coffee pot. They took it upon themselves to introduce me to the rest of the group members as they arrived. All the members arrived at least five minutes early, and we sat down in the family den for our meeting.

This group had obviously bonded into a wonderful community. Over the course of the time we spent together, I learned the men in the group played golf twice a month together, and the women spent every Saturday morning scrapbooking. During the meeting, I could tell they had respect for one another by the way they asked one another questions and commented about the Bible passage.

The meeting ended on time and included an extended time of deep sharing and prayer for each other. Doesn't this sound like a great small group?

In many respects, this group was healthy. But

in one important, life-giving way, it was lacking. This group was not motivated to include outsiders and reminded me of the small group of young married couples I was a part of in the past. From personal experience, their future did not look promising.

During the meeting, I never heard any discussion about relating to people outside the group or a desire to invite others to join. I asked when the last new member joined and was told it was over a year ago when a new member to the church inquired as to where they might find a small group that fit their age group.

It's as if the members of this small group unconsciously decided to close the group to protect the relationships. Or, the deep-knit relationships birthed in the group produced complacency. Regardless of the root issue, it's a recipe for failure. We must give away what God has given us or what we have will just wither away.

Healthy Small Groups Grow!

Oddly enough, just a couple of weeks ago the pastor over this small group called me with an update. He told me that a few months after my visit, the group began to visibly disintegrate. As he spoke with the members, he found two couples in the group knew the group had been deteriorating for quite some time, but they didn't know anything could be done to save it. The couple leading the group didn't want to end it, but a majority of the members were relieved when they were given permission by the pastor to find another group or start a new one.

Throughout the Old Testament, we see that God blessed Israel and then tested them. It's a pattern I see repeated in small groups as well. God blesses us with a love for one another and a sense of belonging. Then the testing comes. Will we be faithful to invite others in to experience what we're now enjoying or sit and soak in the blessing and ignore the reason for the blessing?

When Israel was in the desert following the cloud, God provided manna for them to eat. It fell from the sky each day and would spoil if kept too long. Biblical community is a lot like manna. If you hoard it and don't extend it to the lost and hurting world around you, it will slowly spoil from the inside out because it has a far greater purpose than making a group feel comfortable.

The saddest thing I've ever seen is a small group whose members have been together for many years without a new face in the circle. While they're quite comfortable and know each other very well, they've lost a sense of purpose beyond themselves. After one small group experience that Etna and I endured while visiting yet another church's small group, she commented, "Christ hasn't been welcomed by that group in a long, long time." She was absolutely right. The group we visited had ceased to meet in the name of Jesus many years before. They were only meeting in the name of established, comfortable relationships. Or to put it another way, they met in the name of selfishness. I know this may sound harsh, but if we don't call it by its true name, we'll never deal with the root issue.

Why Focus on Outsiders?

There are lots of good reasons to invite others to your group. The first one is easy to share, because it's one of the last things Jesus said to His disciples. In Matthew 28:19-20, Jesus said:

> "All authority in heaven and on earth has been given to me. Therefore go and make disciples of all nations, baptizing them in the name of the Father and of the Son and of the Holy Spirit,

teaching them to obey everything I have commanded you. And surely I am with you always, to the very end of the age."

At first glance, it looks as if every Christian should instantly become a missionary to China or a rain forest tribe in South America. While thousands of Christians have devoted their lives to foreign missions, we're also responsible to love people into the kingdom of God who work in our office or live in the house next door.

Beyond the simple obedience to Jesus' command, there are a number of additional motivating issues that stir me to include others in my group. Which one motivates you?

Group Preservation - On average, groups that don't grow with new members begin to decline after 8 months. If you enjoy the healthy "family" feeling you're experiencing now, you need to pursue relationships with unchurched people who need what you have already found. For small groups to thrive, they need a sizeable challenge that requires the whole group's participation to remain healthy. Making friends with and involving unchurched people in the life of your small group is hands-down the best way to preserve that family feeling.

Intimacy with God – God is anxious to pour out his Spirit on those who are about His business. If you think your level of intimacy with God is good now, just wait until you begin to reach out to unchurched friends! The love I experience directly from God and indirectly through other members of my small group is always taken to a new level when the small group is focused outward. It has made an overwhelming difference in my life. When I'm giving away what God's given me, it's as if He gives me a continually increasing sense of relationship and unity with Him.

Intimacy with Others – Groups that focus on difficult tasks—tasks that require the whole group to come together as a team to achieve something they can't do as individuals—become very close-knit. They learn to trust one another and appreciate each other's strengths. Without exception, when my small groups have made a collective effort to befriend someone who needs a spiritual family, it's drawn us together and given us a depth of relationship that is hard to describe.

If you've only experienced relationships with other Christians on a friendship or acquaintance level, you're missing out on a level of intimacy that God gives His kids when they're about His business, working as a team.

The Fun Factor – I have personally discovered that my small group's "fun factor" diminishes rapidly when there aren't new people joining the group at least every other month. While life isn't all about fun and games, it sure is attractive to members and visitors alike. If you're like me, the last thing you want to do is to drag yourself to a boring meeting every week that isn't fun. New people, new stories, and new challenges to pray about make a small group fun and meaningful for everyone.

Your Honor, I Object!

I do a lot of small group training around the country. In every crowd, there are one or two people who do not want anything to change in their small group. They don't want to change host homes, nor do they want anyone new to join their group. Apparently, these folks have never experienced this kind of Christian love before and they're afraid they'll lose it! Others don't want to grow and seem to enjoy the static, secure feeling they have in a closed group. Regardless of the motivation, it's not a valid reason to keep a group closed because all closed groups die a slow, painful death.

When I ask these folks why they want a closed group, the main objection I hear is that new people coming in will reduce a small group's level of intimacy. But, as I shared earlier, this "speed bump" on the road to intimacy is temporary and short lived if it happens at all. As new people become regular members of a growing small group, the level of intimacy may operate at a reduced level for a few weeks, but it will *deepen* to a new level quickly. On other side of the coin, new members add so much excitement and "newness" to the group that it's worth any temporary discomfort, if any arises. In some groups, the level of intimacy increases instantly.

When The Going Gets Tough, The Tough Get Grilling!

In our current small group, Etna and I noticed that our group was showing the first signs of stagnation after just two months of being together. Unlike our previous groups, this group began to share transparently from the first meeting onward, and I could see we were moving through the stages of small group life quickly. Our conflict stage was very short and not that rocky. So, we are already familiar with each other's wounds and areas of weakness. We're also mature enough to know that deep emotional wounds don't get healed instantly and that it will take time and support to see transformation. In our opinion, our group was ready to grow to outsiders. We shared our thoughts with the group and they heartily agreed.

As a group, we decided to have a barbeque at our house to launch the process of being outward-focused. As we planned the event during a small group meeting, we didn't talk about food as the first item on the agenda. Instead, we asked each person whom he or she would like to bring to the event, suggesting an unchurched friend or co-worker who lived nearby (versus a friend who lives an hour away due to urban spread and heavy traffic we have here in Houston). Knowing that our friends would come to our home more readily than another member's home, Etna and I had a very long list of people we wanted to invite. Then, we wrote out the list and began to pray for them by name each week as part of our time together.

All of our small group members invited friends, and a couple of their friends showed up. More of our own friends came, which we expected because they'd been to our home before and were comfortable. We asked everyone who told us they'd be there to bring something, even the unchurched folks. After all, this was not a church party. My friends and group members who are always punctual were asked them to bring ice, cups, plates, napkins and utensils, or an appetizer. Those known to float in late were asked to bring dessert.

Our barbeque was a big hit! I'd like to think it was all due to my ability to make the finest smoked brisket in Texas, but I can't take the credit.

Everyone who came brought something and felt like they contributed to the event's success. No one felt like an "honored guest" in our home. Our small group members didn't focus on each other, but invested the afternoon into learning about and relating to people in the house they did not know. It was a fun day, and everyone enjoyed each other. Our strategy, by the way, was to get to know them well enough to invite them to come to a small group meeting or our church's Sunday services.

The next week, we invited all the guests to our small group meeting in hopes we might have a new face in the room. Not one visitor showed up. Some of the group members were disappointed, but I wasn't bothered a bit! Why? Because I've discovered it takes six to eight separate invitations before an unchurched friend will visit my small group. Our barbeque was a good start, but I knew additional dinners, game nights, and activities would be required to form friendships. It will be out of these friendships that conversations about God will naturally occur, and invitations to our small group meetings will be extended and accepted.

Another wonderful side effect of the barbeque was that one of our small group members started talking about the group and inviting her friends.

Our group has grown with two new members in the last few weeks. There's a new excitement in the air during our meetings, and I can tell that our first planned event really changed the mentality of our group members.

Yup, that barbeque was a huge success. And while we're still on the subject, I do make an excellent brisket. Ask anyone who's eaten it and they'll testify to its smoky goodness!

Tanks a lot!

By now, you've read enough to discover I am passionate about Jesus and experiencing His power in small groups. But, you probably don't know that I am also passionate about marine aquariums. I absolutely love them, and have two right now… a large, 150-gallon tank in my office and a smaller 20-gallon tank at home. The office tank is teeming with aquatic life from around the world. The tank at home is designed to house a mated pair of clown fish and a host anemone, just like the movie, *Finding Nemo*.

The hobby is challenging. It's so challenging that I can't imagine attempting it without help from others. So, I have joined a local club of marine aquarium enthusiasts. There are monthly meetings and a web-based forum where we discuss questions and findings in the hobby. We are indeed a bunch of odd people with our own language. Remember those geeks who sat in the cafeteria and made jokes about biology that no one understood? That would be us, all grown up. Within our club, there are people who have accumulated a vast storehouse of knowledge about marine life and those who bought a used fish tank a month ago and have no idea what they're doing. It's a great group in which to be a member.

While cleaning my tank a few years ago, I got a feeling that I was supposed to use my hobby to build relationships with unchurched people. Ever since then, I have worked hard to be helpful to the "newbies" in our group and show them how to set up a tank and learn to be patient while it matures to the point that they can safely add fish and corals.

If one of my coral colonies multiplies, I offer it to someone in the club for a fraction of its retail value or just give it away for free. On many occasions, I too am offered corals from other member's tanks.

Why share this with you? I think it's important for you to consider how you can use your hobbies and interests to connect with unchurched people.

As a member of my club, I am consistently going into the homes of other members. If I see a person who needs a friend, I use our common hobby as a bridge to invite them into my life. I'll offer to help them work on their tank some Saturday and then invite them over to see my tank. When we're getting along as new friends, I'll invite them over for dinner. At that dinner party, I'll invite another couple or family from my small group to join us. This way, my unchurched friends will become acquainted with my small group friends.

By strategically repeating this process of planned interaction over and over, my aquarium club friends will get to know enough of my small group members to feel comfortable in a small group meeting or another barbeque I will host at my home.

If you scrapbook or play golf with others in your small group, invite an unchurched friend to join you. Much of what I shared in chapter two can be applied here, so if your small group has been together for three months and you've bonded as friends, it's the perfect time to begin reaching out.

Events or Relationships?
One might conclude that the way to grow a small

group numerically is to plan lots of parties, but this isn't entirely true. The only reason my friends show up to a party at my house is because we were friends first. We have invested time together in a mutually beneficial, non-judgmental relationship. They have come to know me as a good friend who is deeply concerned about their well-being, wanting nothing in return. I have no hidden agenda. They are not a potential notch on my "salvation belt." It really is a mutual, unconditional friendship.

Most of my unchurched friends have mild to *wild* ideas about God, how He views us, and what He wants from us. Some think He wants more than can or should be given, while others don't think He wants anything. What seems to impact them most is the fact that I don't maintain the attitude that we can only continue our friendship if they begin to believe like I do. Evidently, this is unique among born-again Christians today, which is sad. Jesus was never like that.

In my opinion, many of my unchurched friends are puzzled by my view of God and the deep friendship I maintain with Him. If you were to ask them to describe a typical born-again Christian, they'll be quick to tell you that

Christians are two-faced, hypocritical zealots or no different than anyone else. I work hard to show them that I'm a true friend, one who cares about them and has a love for them that they may not even have for themselves. That's what God wants from us—to spend enough time with those who don't have what we have so they can see Him through us.

A long time ago, I heard a pastor say there are only two reasons why people don't become born-again Christians. The first reason is that they've never met one. The second reason is that they *have* met one and didn't like what they saw!

What 'Widening your Circle' Is Not

As I walked through a mall doing some shopping one Saturday, a young fellow whom I'd never met walked up to me and asked me this question: "If you were to die today and appear before God, and He were to say to you, 'Why should I let you into My heaven?' what would your answer be?" I knew my answer would be, "Because Your Son died for my sins," but I couldn't force my lips to form the words. I was simply bowled over by his approach.

When I think of sharing the love God has given me, it's in the midst of a deep, developing friendship, not approaching total strangers. I'm sure some people feel led to do that, but not me. I'm just not wired that way.

Reaching out to unchurched people outside your small group is all about making friends, praying for their needs as they share them with you, and showing them God's love over the long haul. This is a powerful and fun way to share your faith.

Being Flavorful and Illuminating

In the book of Matthew, we find Jesus preaching to a crowd of followers on the top of a mountain. In the middle of what is most probably his most famous sermon, He said:

> *"You are the salt of the earth. But if the salt loses its saltiness, how can it be made salty again? It is no longer good for anything, except to be thrown out and trampled by men. You are the light of the world. A city on a hill cannot be hidden. Neither do people light a lamp and put it under a bowl. Instead they put it on its stand, and it gives light to everyone in the house. In the same way, let your light shine before men, that they may see your good deeds and praise your Father in heaven"* (Matthew 5:13-16).

I believe Jesus chose the examples of salt and light with great care.

Salt is a preservative and a seasoning, so it has two applications for your small group. When you act as salt of the earth for God's kingdom, you are preserving what Jesus did here thousands of years ago. When salt is used as a seasoning, it draws additional flavor out of most foods. Your group has a spice that does not overpower, but enhances what is already present! Just being you when involving others is being the salt of the earth.

When Jesus told His followers they were to be the light of the world, He was helping them understand that the world is filled with darkness—the absence of light—and their knowledge of Him and belief that He was the Messiah was illumination. In those days, the only light they had at night was from the flame of an oil lantern. Oil was expensive, so no one would light a lamp and waste it. So, His words in verse 15 are just stating the obvious to the crowd. He said, *"Neither do people light a lamp and put it under a bowl. Instead they put it on its stand, and it gives light to everyone in the house."*

Extending God's love to unchurched people is what your small group is all about and is the very heart of God. If you adopt this attitude, you'll discover that being a member of your small group is far more than just a weekly meeting. Small group will become a powerful way of life, and you'll see God's hand at work in your own life as well as the other members of your group. Don't hide what God has given you. Let it shine so all can enjoy it!

Apply it!
- Hurting people are all around us, but we're often too busy to see them and care enough to reach out. During your prayer time each day, ask God to give you a new set of eyes for all those around you who don't fully realize His love and desire to relate to them as their heavenly Father.
- Pray for your unchurched friends by name each day and the unchurched friends of others in your small group. Make a list and keep it in your Bible.
- Start thinking. In what ways can you deepen your friendships with your unchurched friends?

Share it!
- Throw a party in your home, and invite all your unchurched friends as well as at least three or four people from your small group to come. Ask

everyone invited (especially your unchurched friends) to bring something for the meal so they feel as if they are contributing. During the party itself, insure all the small group members spend time with people they do not know. If you can't think of things to do at this party, consider playing board games together or watch a ball game or movie together. Pray for this party in the weeks leading up to it, and ask God to give your invited small group members the boldness needed to talk to and befriend your unchurched friends.

- Be salt and light to the world around you! If one of your unbelieving friends shares a need, serve them. If they have a medical, relational, or financial problem beyond your ability to serve, be bold enough to tell them you'll be praying for them, asking God to bring healing or a solution. Follow up in the weeks to come and make sure they know you have been praying daily for their need. (The more you are praying for God's heart for people, the easier doing this becomes. After a while, it will be second nature, and your unchurched friends won't think you're a religious freak…just someone who cares enough to pray on their behalf.) Friends care, and serving and praying is how you can show you care in a powerful new way.

Additional Reading
Conspiracy of Kindness – Steve Sjogren
Are You Fishing With A Net? – Randall Neighbour

Chapter 5
Leaving Home

On my bookshelf I keep a little booklet entitled *Leaving Home* by Michael Mack. In the introduction of this booklet, Mack describes a "happy" Christian family. The parents, both in their late sixties, have been married for 42 years and continue to work full-time jobs. The dad works on the loading dock of a trucking company and the mom works at a fast food restaurant. Their three children, Hank, Millie, and Kenneth are all college graduates and obviously intelligent individuals. The whole family loves Jesus and they are faithful church members.

The writer goes on to describe each child. Hank just turned 40 and enjoys writing science fiction stories in his room, which he shares with his brother, Kenneth. Millie, now 36, has always been very helpful around the house and feeds and bathes the family dog. Kenneth, the youngest at 33, is quite the athlete and enjoys playing baseball, basketball and soccer.

What a messed-up family! The parents have not taught their children to be productive adults and to gain independence. The children, all in their thirties or forties, have no desire to start a family and move out of their parent's home.

What's needed here is for a loving friend to sit down with that whole family and explain to them how unhealthy their family has become and to challenge them to make some radical changes, right? That's exactly how this story develops. A close friend tells the mother how dysfunctional the family has been and works with her to make changes that will bring health to the situation.

Same Song, Second Verse

In church life, the exact same story could be told about many a small group. The group has been together for a long, long time. The members, not knowing they are to grow up and leave the group, are happy to stay. The similarities to the family described above are downright frightening!

Let me be the one who shares how you—a maturing small group member—can grow up spiritually and move beyond your current small group experiences. Your current small group may feel warm and cozy, but God never leaves us to stagnate in our comfort zones. He challenges us to step up and participate in starting new spiritual families.

While you may not be motivated to move out of your current group experience, it may be on your horizon! It's just the next natural thing one does after serving as a caring, small group member. It's one sign of maturity and spiritual health.

When you adopt a prayer life, deep friendships with members *and* unchurched people as I've encouraged you to do thus far in this book, you will see how easy it will be to take this next step. God may use you to start your own group. He might invite you to be a part of a team that starts a group in a different part of your town. He might use you through a new group to reach people that are not currently being reached. The possibilities are numerous.

Myths About Leadership

Leading a small group is the most rewarding thing my wife and I do. One of the things I enjoy the most is developing others to lead their own groups. I've helped dozens of small group members become leaders. Each person has concerns about taking on the role and reasons as to why they are not qualified or ready for leadership. They believe various things about small group leadership that are only half-truths or completely not true whatsoever. Here are some of them.

"I don't have the time to lead a small group."
Truthfully, leading a small group will take more
time out of your schedule than being a member,
but it doesn't *feel* like a huge time sacrifice
because it should be what you know God wants
you to do next. It all goes back to priorities or
the "big rocks in the jar of life" I mentioned earlier.

Etna and I led a small group where one of
the members was always too busy with work on
Thursday nights to attend meetings. Allen
owned his own computer service business and
was always working nights, when companies did-
n't need their networks operating at full speed.

Initially, I didn't think Allen would make the
time for membership, let alone leadership. But,
he sensed God's call on his life for leading a small
group and shared it with me. He attended the
training at our church and I asked him to assist
me in our group, which he made the time to do.
It was only a year later that he took over my
group as we moved out to launch a new one.

When Allen began to ask God what the next
part of small group life was for him, God said
"move into leadership." If you hear God telling
you it's time to move into leadership, don't worry

about the time issue. The time factor always balances out when you're doing God's will.

"I don't have it all together. How could I become a leader?"

Let's face it. We all have areas of our life that still need healing or work. Jesus developed young, ignorant fishermen into world changers, and that allows just about anyone who wants to lead the opportunity, if they're willing to work toward it. If you don't feel spiritually mature enough to lead a group, ask someone more spiritually mature in your group to help you grow. If you're struggling in one area or another, tell someone and get some help! Even if your motivation is not to grow into a leader, it's important to grow spiritually. As you grow, you'll see opportunities to lead. Just keep growing and don't let anyone tell you you're not good enough or will never be good enough to become a small group leader. Anyone with a heart for people can lead a small group of some kind.

"I don't have an outgoing personality."

Personally speaking, my outgoing personality seems to get me in more trouble than a shy person could imagine! I often speak without thinking, and

I'm always finding out I must continue to work on my listening skills. In my small group meetings, I have to force myself to be quiet and focus on others.

Introverts (shy or contemplative personalities) are often far better at small group leadership because they naturally listen better than someone like me. Research has shown that *any* kind of personality type can produce an excellent small group leader as long as the person behind the personality is willing to love others and be a true friend. Personality has little to do with leadership. It's all about how much a person cares about others.

Remember the story I just shared about Allen? Just about a year after I turned our group over to Allen, he turned it over to a young college co-ed who was as shy and timid as one could imagine. She loved God and had a heart for people, and this is all she needed to befriend and love those in her group!

"I get all choked up when I have to speak publicly." Fortunately, small group leadership is all about loving people and not about possessing incredible public speaking skills. Because I spend lots of time with my fellow small group members between

meetings, our official weekly meetings feel more like a bunch of friends getting together to sing, pray, and share our lives. Good small group leaders don't do all the talking during meetings. They ask good questions when needed and encourage others in the room to share by not doing a majority of the speaking. Focusing on deepening the relationships between members is what leadership is all about. In fact, if you're lousy at public speaking it's a bonus to being an excellent small group leader.

Grow up!

When you sense God's call on you to lead, there are a few important things you should do before you actually get a group of your own.

Walk in Spiritual Maturity

Your walk with Christ is the first qualification for becoming a spiritual leader in your church. How is your intimacy with Jesus? Is He your best friend? Do you trust Him? Do you hear His voice? These are basic questions that provide the foundation for leading others.

It is from this kind of intimacy with Jesus that He begins to minister through you. Does He flow through you in ministry to others? Do you hear

God's leading in how to minister to people in the small group meetings? Do you sense what the Spirit is doing through the group? You may not have the experience at hearing God like your small group leader, but you should be learning to flow with what God is doing in your group.

Walking in spiritual maturity also means that you are free from habitual sins that control your thoughts and actions. I am not saying that you have to be perfect, but it is important to allow the Lord to deal with secret sins or sinful patterns that are out of control before you enter into leadership.

Is your thought life under control? Do you do secret things that cause you great shame? Do you treat your kids in a godly way? Is your marriage strong? Talk with your small group leader or your pastor if you have any concerns about things that the Spirit might be revealing to you right now. He wants you to walk in spiritual freedom so that you can help others walk in the same freedom!

Take Ownership In Your Group

If you are serious about leading a group in the future, start acting like a good small group leader, even though you haven't been formally asked. Call your small group leader and ask them if you can help out with some aspect of small group life such as hosting the meeting, organizing a party for the group, or leading part of the meeting. In addition, start calling other members of your group to see how their week is going and pray for them on the phone.

Keep this up and the leader of your group will be talking about you favorably when he or she meets with your pastor or your group's coach. If your motives are godly and you're willing to do whatever is asked of you, you'll probably get an invitation to join the leadership team sooner than you think.

Focus on Unchurched People

Another key thing you should do is to relate to the unchurched people you meet at your group's parties, even if they are the friends of other members. The goal isn't to steal the friendship, but to create a network of friendships for the unchurched people attached to your group.

When numerous friendships form, unchurched people will feel comfortable enough to join your group. Spending time with unchurched people will also make you feel very close to God because it provides a contrast of beliefs between what you know about God and unbelievers may not know.

To illustrate this, compare yourself to a candle, shining in the noonday sun, (among very mature believers all the time). In that setting, your light doesn't seem to burn very brightly for God. But go into a dark room, (surrounded by people who do not have the "Light of the World" residing within them), and you'll feel very brightly lit indeed!

Reaching out to unchurched people through friendship is an important part of group membership. Most churches want to see this value in future leaders.

Contact your group's coach or pastor in charge of small groups

Most small group leaders have a special relationship with the pastor over small groups at their church and/or a small group coach. When you feel called to lead a small group, ask your group's coach or your pastor if you can visit with them about your desire to move into small group leadership. Of course, you'll need to discuss this with your own small group leader first, so it doesn't come as a surprise!

Let your coach or pastor know you're willing to learn as a member and need their help, as well as the help of your small group leader, in any area you need to work on to grow into the role.

If you'll take the time to do these three things, you'll probably be leading a group of your own within a year or less. The only thing that may hold you back is an unwillingness to deal with problems brought to your attention by your leadership. If concerns are raised, work hard not to take offense. See it as an opportunity to grow and mature in Christ.

Small Group Success: Turning Members Into Ministers

When it comes to small groups of Christians meeting together in Jesus' name, moving members into ministry is one of the main goals. The more trained and motivated ministers a church has, the more small groups it can have. This results in more people being involved in relationships that are powerful and transformational. Success for any church is not based on the size of their small groups nor the number of small groups. It's based on the church's ability to help every church member become spiritually mature enough to look in the mirror and see themselves as a minister.

To be called ministers, we must have a ministry, right? Our ministry as small group members is to love others and show them Christ through our lifestyle. When we begin to do this well, we need to show others how to do it. That's small group leadership. It's not really that hard to grasp, and it should not be anything that causes concern or reluctance on your part. It's just the next step in spiritual maturity.

I began this chapter with an illustration about an odd family whose adult children never moved out of the house. Work hard not to be like this! Pray about how God wants to shape you into a future small group leader and the way you'll lead others through friendship and into ministry. Help your small group leader with anything they ask of you, and take ownership of your group by pitching in to serve others.

Soon enough, you'll be moving out of your current spiritual house to make a new one of your own! Begin to develop leadership skills now while you're still a member, remembering that the best leadership skills are being a friend, a good listener, and one who cares enough to pray and invest time into other members.

Apply it!
- Share with your small group leader that you know leadership is in your future. Begin to act like a good small group leader by focusing on the things a good leader does between meetings—spend time with other members laughing, eating, praying, and relating to their unchurched friends.

Share it!
- Many times, we don't see the potential in ourselves. So, if you can see leadership potential in another small group member, encourage them to pursue it. Brag about their love for people and willingness to serve in upcoming small group meetings and tell your small group leader they'd make an excellent assistant leader. Pray daily for them to see what you see, and then help them develop as a leader, even if you're not feeling as if you should become a leader alongside them.

Additional Reading
8 Habits of Effective Small Group Leaders
- Dave Earley
Leading from the Heart - Michael Mack
Answers to Your Cell Group Questions
- Randall Neighbour

Chapter 6
Your Weekly Meeting

If I were to ask you if adding just one more weekly meeting would give you a sense of fulfillment in life, you'd probably think I've lost my mind, right? We live in a busy society chock full of meetings and things to do. One more meeting would only make life more stressful, not meaningful! For small group gatherings to be more than a meeting, it must be an exciting time of discovering God in a fresh new way. They must move beyond the realm of a meeting we "must" attend to a gathering that we "long" to attend because we know God will show up. Let me illustrate the difference:

As I prayed about what our group should discuss in an upcoming meeting, God impressed upon me to separate the men and women after worship for a time of sharing and prayer for one another. My church supplied us with an outline for the evening, and we were asked to apply what we were learning through our pastor's sermon series on the Ten Commandments.

That night, we began with a time of worship. After the second song, someone prayed and acknowledged Christ's presence with us, based on Matthew 18:20 where Jesus said, *"Where two or three come together in my name, there am I with them."* When we sang the last song, I really felt the presence of God in the room with us.

The men moved into a small room that the host used as a home office and the ladies stayed in the living room for our discussion and ministry time. As I read the Ten Commandments, I asked the guys to ask God where they might have broken one or more of the commandments in the past week. This was not an inappropriate question for this group, because we knew each other well and had been together for six months.

One man shared that he didn't kill anyone last week, or any other week for that matter, but he did visualize running someone off the road for cutting him off on his way home from work. Another shared that he was not completely truthful to his wife about his life before marriage. Though he knew it wasn't from last week, he felt led to confess it.

Then a very good friend of mine shared as he stared at the floor. Anthony gave a heavy sigh and said, "I never really thought what I am about to tell you was wrong, but God is showing me right now

I need to confess it as sin and make it right."

It was quiet in the room for a few seconds, and we waited for Anthony to continue.

"I have been padding my billed hours to two of my customers for over a year because they always pay their bills without question. I justified it because on occasion, I do work for them and don't bill them for all the hours I should, but I know I've made more than my fair share."

As you can imagine, we could have heard a pin drop in that room! I asked Anthony if he wanted to pray and confess that sin to God and receive His forgiveness. We could tell it was hard for him to do because he struggled to form the words. A guy sitting near him put his hand on his shoulder when he prayed. When he was finished, another said, "You are forgiven."

Then I asked Anthony what he knew God would want him to do to make it right. He said, "I need to go to both of these companies and ask if I can pay them back or work for free for a number of hours to make it up. But I'm scared to do it. I just might lose the accounts or worse. I could get thrown in jail."

Because of Anthony's transparency, three other guys in my group confessed sin and prayed.

After the meeting, an older man from our group asked Anthony to walk around the block with him. He told him to trust the Lord and be obedient. Anthony agreed to meet with the company owners and talk with them that very week and report back about what happened.

A few days later, Anthony called me to say that both the business owners were stunned that he'd be so honest with them without being accused of stealing beforehand. One owner said he thought it might be happening and was about to suspend the contract based on suspicion. To Anthony's surprise, one of the owners said he could work it off and that would be the end of it. The other said they could call it even, but he would lose the account.

This small group gathering was anything but another weekly meeting, wasn't it? God showed up in power and we all sensed it. People shared deep issues and were transparent, and we saw God glorified. We not only discussed a truth from the Bible; we applied it to our lives.

The effects didn't stop at the meeting either. The members held one another accountable to do the right thing in the days afterward, and it was a transformational time for all of us, especially Anthony.

Focusing on Christ in the Midst

Lots of small groups gather in the name of being together, to study and/or apply the Bible, for prayer and ministry, or to work through a book on an aspect of the Christian life. But for a small group to be powerful to the point of personal transformation, each member must come with a desire to focus on the presence, power, and purpose of Christ.

The Presence of Christ

Many groups get bogged down in trying to fix one another's problems or just study the Bible like a textbook. If a group of people gather regularly in Christ's name and invite Him to be in their midst and work powerfully through them, He will! This is why it's so important to walk into the door of the home or room where your small group meets with a holy expectation. When Jesus walked the streets of Jerusalem, people quickly discovered He was not like the many false messiahs who preceded Him. He was the true Christ, the one and only Son of God. It was in His presence that they found healing and discovered a directional purpose in life. If a small group gathers for any other reason than to be in Christ's presence, they'll miss the powerful opportunity that God has for them.

The Power of Christ

The Holy Spirit dwells within every born-again Christian. When we meet in the name of the Lord, versus our own agenda, need, or topic of interest, we can experience the powerful, transformation of Christ in our midst. If you've never prayed for another small group member and felt moved to give them a hug from God or share an impression or word of encouragement you've received from God, you're missing out on one of the best parts of small group life!

I have a friend named Christi who made a decision to follow God two years ago. While she's had her fair share of setbacks in her new life in Christ, she is excited about her new spiritual family and frequently brings friends to the meetings.

One night, her friend Susan came with her. During our time of prayer for one another, Susan boldly shared that she was hurting over the loss of her son, who was taken from her by Child Protective Services due to her alcoholism and neglect. When she asked for prayer, Christi was the first to say, "I'd like to pray for you. Would that be OK?"

As Christi began to pray, Susan began to sob, then cry hard. After Christi finished praying, she said, "Susan, God loves you and knows your love for your son. But you have to take ownership of your alcoholism and see where you've tried to find happiness in a bottle instead of looking to God."

Christi would be the first to tell you she is not a spiritual giant. But, that night she heard from God and encouraged her friend in a powerful time of prayer and healing.

God desires to work through His children to extend the power to heal and restore. When you take part in your small group meetings, ask God to use you mightily and expect it! Also expect God to work mightily through others. It's just as important to receive ministry as it is to give it away. While God works miraculously in unexplained ways, He just loves to work through His children because it is a blessing to the giver and the receiver.

The Purpose of Christ

When we get to heaven, we'll have an eternity to enjoy one another's company and worship God face to face. Here on earth, we have been given a challenge to share our lives, transformed by Christ, with as many unbelievers as possible!

Invest time in every small group meeting to pray for unchurched friends and for God to condition your heart to love people the way He does. If your group isn't strategically planning ways to connect group members with unchurched friends, take the lead by throwing a party and challenging every member to bring an unchurched friend.

Show Up for the Meetings

In one of my small groups, we had a fellow who turned up five minutes before the meetings started and sat there like a bump on a log. He rarely shared anything about himself, didn't sing with us, and never prayed for anyone, let alone his own concerns or issues. I'll never forget this fellow. He clearly taught me that "showing up" for meetings includes far more than attendance!

When you go to your weekly small group meeting, bring your mind and your heart with you and plan to edify or "build up" others, as well as receive ministry. God wants to use you in powerful ways in the lives of the other members of your group. God also wants to use the other members of the group to build you up, so don't hold back when you're hurting. Share your needs transparently with the group so they can pray for you and help you find the root of your issue.

Your Meeting is a Time of Discovery

I have visited many small groups where the entire ministry to its members is compressed into one two-hour meeting each week. Those who share a need and receive prayer may receive ten minutes' worth of the group's time during the meeting and little to no follow-up until the next week when the group meets. A growing, healthy small group of believers discovers needs during meetings and then continues that ministry to completion in the six days and 22 hours between future meetings.

Before you walk into the room where your next small group will meet, ask the Lord to let you discover a need of another member that you can meet outside of the meeting. Then look and listen for your cue. Inevitably, someone will share a need that requires prayer. It may be that you can serve them in the days to follow to show them Christ's love. If not, then make a conscious decision to pray for them daily and call them to let them know you're interceding on their behalf. When you call, ask them if they would appreciate it if you dropped by one evening to pray with them. When a small group of believers cares enough to pray and serve each other between meetings, it makes all the difference in the world. If no one does this in your group, be the first and raise the bar for involvement.

How to Pray and Minister To Others During Your Meeting

Each week, I have the opportunity to pray for other members of my small group. When it comes time to pray, I always take a deep breath and ask myself the following question: "Am I about to pray a nice, rehearsed prayer or do I know without a doubt that I'm about to pray something that God has given me that will be powerful?"

This stops me cold most of the time. My head is often filled with trite thoughts and earthly advice given in the form of a prayer for a person, and that's the last thing they need! So, I hold back and ask God to tell me how to pray for them. If I don't hear anything, I remain silent.

When I do hear God's prompting, I go ahead and pray aloud or share what I need to share with the person. If you don't know the difference between your own voice and God's, just remember that when God give you the words, it's powerful. You'll know it, the group will know it, and the person receiving it will know it!

Just remember to speak or pray the truth in

love. Often, I know exactly what God would want to say to a person, but my attitude toward him or her is not right and it would only come out as a harsh criticism or condemnation. In these instances, I don't share, but ask God to speak to the person directly and use others who can deliver the message in love.

About once a month, I hear God say to me, "Someone has a word of encouragement for this person, but it's not you." I'm always faithful to risk telling our small group that I believe someone has a word of encouragement for the person, but is holding back.

In most cases, this is true. Someone has something powerful to share or pray over the person in need, but is too scared to do it. This gives them permission to share it during the meeting, be it right or wrong. Or, they call or meet the person between meetings and share what God has given them.

In other cases, I totally confuse the voice of God with the rumbling in my stomach from the extra slice of pizza I had for dinner. That's why it's so important for the small group to have permission to say, "I don't think that was the Spirit of God talking to you, Randall." Believe it or not, this still happens to me because I'm always learning about hearing God's voice!

If this whole subject of hearing the voice of God is foreign territory to you, just start asking God to speak to you each day when you spend time with Him. He's always been a great communicator, and He'll most certainly begin to speak to you through His written Word (the Bible), through other believers, and as thoughts that pop into your head and you know they could not have come from you.

Just remember this rule of thumb. God never contradicts Himself. So, if you think you hear God's voice about something or receive a word of encouragement for someone in your group, insure it doesn't go against the Bible and your small group agrees that it's from God.

The Listening to Speaking Ratio

God gave us two ears and one mouth. I get the distinct impression from our Creator that, by simple design, we're not supposed to use our mouth nearly as much as we're encouraged to use our ears. Throughout the Bible, one can easily find numerous examples of the trouble people find themselves in when they talked too much. I can't find any

instances in the Bible where someone *listened* too much though!

When you're taking part in the ministry time or application of God's Word in your meetings, actively listen to what others are saying. What are they revealing about themselves and how they view

God? What can you learn from them? What needs are they sharing that you can act upon in the days to come?

I am a certified motor mouth. I love to talk and tell jokes and be the life of the party. But when it comes to my fellow small group members, I work hard to listen twice as much as I speak. I can't say I've cured my problem completely, but I make a conscious effort each week to focus on others, not what I want to say next. It takes practice, but those who listen and ask God to reveal needs always receive a powerful ministry outlet that will bless and encourage others when it is time to act or speak.

Bring A Guest

Are your meetings filled with laughter and interaction? This is exactly what people are looking for in our world. The relationships offered by the world are usually shallow and meaningless, where one person wants something from another person and friendship is offered conditionally. Your small group can be an oasis of God's love for these folks!

Don't assume your friends and co-workers will judge you or label you as a fanatic when you ask them to come to an upcoming small group. Just begin to share how much fun you have at meetings, how valuable you are finding the relationships, and how different your small group is compared to a church service.

My unchurched friends usually ask me how it's going or how I'm doing when we talk. It's how people typically begin a conversation. If your friends ask you this, just tell them you're having a great week due to the time you had with the other members of your small group. Ask them if they're a part of a small group, and when they say they're not, invite them to come with you to the next meeting.

Few unchurched people I know want to study the Bible, so I don't describe my small group in this way. This is true because we don't just study the Bible; we interact with it and apply it to our daily lives. I talk about the friendships I've made, how valuable the time is each week and how loved I feel when I leave the meetings. This is what people are searching for, whether they'll come right out and tell you or keep it a secret!

If you will muster up the courage to talk about your small group relationships at the office and with your unchurched friends and neighbors, you'll find they'll soon see you have something they don't have. When you lay down this kind of foundation, you'll feel comfortable inviting them to an upcoming meeting or a party your small group is holding to connect with them.

Just do it! Start "testifying" as to how great the friendships are that you've formed in your small group. Those around you who don't enjoy Christian community will be drawn to it like bugs to a street lamp.

Hosting The Meeting

If you've never hosted your small group in your home, I highly recommend it! Even if you live in a tiny efficiency apartment and your fellow small group members will have to sit on the floor or bring a folding chair with them, it will be great! I've sat on hard wood floors many times during small group, and have seen God move powerfully in our midst.

There are a few things you need to know about hosting a meeting in your home. Some are practical considerations and others are spiritual.

Before the Group Arrives

Is the group meeting at your home this week? The day before the actual meeting, vacuum the floors in the room where the meeting will be held. If you do it a few minutes before members arrive, the dust a typical vacuum cleaner creates may affect some people. Etna and I also look around the public areas of our home and move stray papers, shoes, and cups that seem to accumulate in our den.

Just before guests arrive, move the chairs or couches in your main room into a circle. We always bring in dining room chairs to insure there's enough room for everyone plus a few visitors. Position the chairs and couches close together to make for an intimate gathering, and make the circle wide enough so that no person feels they have permission to sit outside the circle.

Also, find a box of tissue and set it on a side table or your coffee table. This way, you won't have to search the house during ministry time if someone needs one. While we're on the subject of tissue, do remember to put a fresh roll of toilet paper in the bathroom and tidy up in there, too!

I also try to remember to turn off or unplug the phone extensions in the part of the house where we're meeting, and turn down the volume on the message machine. This way, telemarketers and friends who call during the meeting won't distract me or other members from the incessant ringing they hear.

Etna and I always try to provide refreshments when the group meets in our home. We put on a pot of coffee and set out some chips, salsa, wedges of cheese, and crackers. Because our small group has "refrigerator rights" in our home, they know where to find soft drinks. If this is a financial stretch for you, just ask your small group leader to help you contact other members and ask them to bring something to contribute.

If you have a dog or cat that will bother a member (allergies, a strong dislike or fear of certain kinds of pets, etc.) be sure to put them outside or in a spare room for the evening. Our golden retriever just loves our group and it's not a problem, but if a visitor is invited that would not appreciate the constant requests Lady makes for attention during a meeting, we'd gladly put her in another room. We love our dog, but we love to see our small group worship freely and grow even more.

There are two other very important things you must do before your small group members arrive. Work on the physical and spiritual climate of your home. Insure that it's cool or warm enough in your home by adjusting your thermostat. Remember that your house will be filled with people and the collective body heat will raise the thermometer within 20 minutes of the meeting's official starting time.

To adjust the spiritual temperature of your home, take five minutes to sit in the room where you will meet and ask God to fill your home with His peace, leaving no room for anything evil such as strife or discord. Invite Him to come in power during the meeting. Sometimes, I will play praise music softly and pray for each member by name, asking God to touch him or her in a special way that night. If you've ever walked into a room and felt you could cut the tension in the air with a knife, you can rest assured that no one prayed like this before you arrived. I've forgotten to pray through my home before a meeting and I saw a dynamic drop in the level of sharing and ministry the group experienced that night.

During the Meeting

As the host for the evening, I make sure everyone is comfortable in my home. I'm not entertaining on these nights, but I do feel a need to offer hospitality. If everyone is feeling fine with the temperature, but I see one woman shivering, I ask if she'd like a shawl or blanket from our TV room. If everyone is warm, I quietly slip out and turn down the air conditioning a degree or two.

After the Meeting

When the concluding prayer is offered, Etna is always zipping off to the kitchen to ensure the snacks are ready and that the ice bucket is full so folks can congregate in that area of the house to fellowship. We always encourage people to hang around for a while and visit, because that's what good friends do! Good friends are also helpful, so I have no problem asking a couple of guys to help me move the couch back in place and chairs back to the dining room.

When everyone is gone, Etna and I lock the doors and turn off the lights. As we're doing it, we're praying through the house again, asking God to fill it with His presence and leave no room for anything that doesn't belong. Why? We encourage our small group members to share hurts with the group. We urge them to confess sins to another person in the group, or at the very least, silently to God during our time of worship.

Please take note of our motivation for praying through the rooms of our home after meetings. We don't do this out of fear, because we have nothing to fear. We just want God to be ever-present in our home.

I know that praying through your home before

and after a small group meeting may sound weird or fanatical to you, but it's hard to argue with scripture. Ephesians 6:12 says, *"For our struggle is not against flesh and blood, but against the rulers, against the authorities, against the powers of this dark world and against the spiritual forces of evil in the heavenly realms."* We can always feel the difference in our home when we pray through it, for the "powers of this dark world" just can't stand to be in a "Son room" like our home!

It's Eleven o'clock! What Now?
On occasion, I'm told by one of my small group members that someone from our group, or a lonely visitor stuck around the host home far too long after everyone else had left. When this happens to me, I simply tell them that we have to be up early and it's past our bedtime already. Often, I share this with them as I am walking them to the door!

On rare occasion, someone will not get this overt hint and still keep talking! So, I put my hand on their shoulder and say, "Can I pray a prayer of blessing over you as you leave?" I guess some people just need a benediction to know when its time to head out the door, and this always works!

It's important to recognize this as a sign that

this person is lonely or has something heavy to share and can't get around to it easily. Follow up with them in the days to come and ask them if they were the last person out the door because they needed to talk about something specific that you just didn't grasp that night. If the person did stay late to discuss a heavy issue with you, it's not wrong to tell them that you need to set a time to talk with them more and pray with them about it versus trying to get it all out late at night. Just remember that your small group leader is available and if you don't know what to do, give him or her a call.

Your Kids Need a Role Model, Not a Babysitter

In conferences and training seminars, I'm often asked the question, "What should we do with our kids during small group meetings?"

I'm a big believer that if we ask the wrong questions, we'll get the wrong answers. The question I would rather answer is, "How can we involve our children in the life of our small group, as well as our weekly meetings?"

Our children are deeply loved by God and desperately need what the small group offers. They'll never discover how important it is to share one's heart and receive ministry unless they are in the room to see it happen!

So, work hard to involve your children in your small group meetings. Invite them to join you in worship, and sing a song or two they know. Train them to play quietly in the middle of the circle, and ask all the small group members to help you with them during the meetings.

Typically, the children are not the problem. It's the parents who feel they won't get anything out of the meeting if forced to watch their children throughout it. This is why it's so important for the whole group to adopt the children as little ones whom God loves deeply and begin to care for them as a parent would do.

In some small groups, a few of the parents take the toddlers to another part of the house to play and the grade school kids to yet another room to pray for one another and talk about what is going on in their world. There's nothing wrong with doing this, and I encourage you to continue it. But, the more your children see you praying for others and being prayed for, the more they will do this themselves.

Our children are not the church of tomorrow. They are the church of today! If we hold to the thought that they are tomorrow's church, most will go into the world and never return. We're seeing the results of that right now in our culture. Radical change is necessary if we wish to see our children be the church! It begins with our modeling biblical community for them today and inviting them to join us in truly loving others with Christ's love.

What's Said in the Meeting
Stays in the Meeting

There's a story about a small group who had developed a deep level of transparent sharing with one another. One night the ministry question was, "What is your greatest struggle today?"

Each person shared honestly and it was turning into an awesome time of transparency. The leader just knew the ministry time to follow would be powerful. Then the last person shared, saying, "My greatest struggle is gossip, and I just can't wait to get out of here!"

All jokes aside, I feel it's important to end this chapter with a word about confidentiality. Gossip, even in the form of a prayer request on behalf of another member, is damaging beyond one's wildest understanding. Your small group is probably the only place where people will share their hurts, expecting others to love them unconditionally. Part of truly loving the other members in your group is not sharing their words, thoughts, or feelings with others.

So, what is shared in your group should stay in that meeting. If a member wasn't there one week and wants to catch up on what went on, feel free to share with them what you alone shared, but that's all you should share. If they want every participant's prayer requests, let them call each person who was at the meeting and ask them directly.

If someone shares something they have done that is harmful to others which requires immediate action to make it right, challenge them right then and there to do what's right in the eyes of God and man. Tell them you'll go along with them for support. If they refuse, be assured that your small group leader will deal with it immediately.

I've heard horror stories about Christians who share other people's secrets and struggles in churches, and it's probably the single greatest reason unchurched people are not a part of a church and following God. Don't fall into this trap with your small group.

Each week, I ask God to take away any memories of what has been shared that I can't pray over and use as fuel to minister to the person in love. He's always faithful and I highly recommend that you do the same.

Apply it!
- Consider the needs of each member of your small group and pray for them each day. Call one or two this week to tell them you are praying for them. If they share something deep with you, encourage them to share it with the group when you next meet, if they feel comfortable enough to do it.
- Prepare your heart for your next meeting. Ask God to speak through you in a powerful way. Ask for ears to hear deep things others share and to know when to speak and when to remain silent.
- During the worship time in your next meeting, welcome Christ into your midst and give Him permission to come in power and show you His purposes for your lives.

Share it!
- Invite a co-worker, family member, or a neighbor to come to your small group when it next meets. The more you ask, the better your chances will be they will say yes, so don't become discouraged.

Give God time to work in their hearts by asking them once a month for six months and watch them change right before your eyes!

- Encourage others in your group when you know they have shared something from the very heart of God, something that could not be considered earthly wisdom or human advice. Pray with other members in your group as often as you can, and ask God to pour Himself out on them in a fresh, powerful way.

- Open your home for an upcoming group meeting. Invite your unchurched friends to come as well!

Additional Reading
Reconnecting the Generations – Daphne Kirk
What Shall We Do With the Children? – An Audio Series by Daphne Kirk
The Shepherd's Guidebook –Ralph Neighbour, Jr.

Chapter 7
Community As a Way of Life

As a kid, I listened to my dad preach a sermon series that helped me understand the importance of living in biblical community with other believers. Here's a brief overview of what I learned.

There are three aspects to our salvation, best described as two points and a process in between. The first point is the important decision to follow God and give Him our lives through the work of the cross. At this life-changing time in our spiritual lives, we are released from the *penalty* of sin, which is death. Praise God! We can look forward to a wonderful life with God after our mortal bodies die.

The second point goes right along with the first. We live in a sinful place and we're tempted to sin all the time. When we leave this place to be with God, we will not have to withstand temptation any longer. This second point is that we will one day be released from the *presence* of sin. Forgive me for being repetitious, but praise God…again! I can't wait to be free from sin. We all have a lot to look forward to when we consider the continuation of our life in Heaven with God.

But there's a lot of years on earth in between these points, right? That's where living in biblical community becomes so vitally important. In Philippians 2:13, we see a challenge set forth by the Apostle Paul:

> *Therefore, my dear friends, as you have always obeyed—not only in my presence, but now much more in my absence—continue to work out your salvation with fear and trembling, for it is God who works in you to will and to act according to his good purpose.*

The third aspect of our salvation is the *process* of "working out our salvation" together. As a point of clarification, let me say that salvation (the first and last points) are a free gift from God. There's nothing we can do to earn it or to deserve it on our own. But once we get it, we're encouraged to live among each other in such a way as to help each other live as an example to those who don't yet know God and to find protection from falling back into sin.

From the time I was 18 until I was just about to turn 24, I abandoned this aspect of my relationship with God. I went my own way, out of biblical community, and tried to do it alone. When I realized the world was a lonely place, I tried to duplicate what I had grown to love, my community of believers who cared for me and loved me.

What I discovered was that everyone is looking for a community where they can be loved unconditionally, but it's impossible to do without the Author of Love! The best I could find was a dumpy little tavern where people listened to one another's problems and had no solutions to offer except to buy them a drink.

When I came back to the church, I rediscovered the power of biblical community. There I found healing for my wounds and a surge of God's Spirit flowing through me to others, who needed a touch by God in the worst way. It gave me a clear sense of purpose in life! Now I know why I am on this planet, why God made me the way He did. I cannot do this alone. God made me to live out my purpose with others of the same mindset. Who are the others? You guessed, it, my small group.

A Lifestyle of Love

In John 15:13, Jesus said: *"Greater love has no one than this, that he lay down his life for his friends."* This was a bold statement. Jesus was both commanding them to love one another with a sacrificial love, but also foreshadowing his own death on a cross so they would not have to experience an eternal separation from God.

When I think about my involvement in my small group, I often think of this verse, and consider the One who powerfully demonstrated it as my source of motivation. If Christ could die for me as a sign of true friendship, I should easily be able to make the others in my group a priority in life.

A couple of weeks ago, I was driving home and thought, "I'll just crawl into bed when I get home. Our small group will get along fine tonight without me at the meeting." I was too tired to even eat that night. If you knew me, you'd know that meant I was really exhausted!

Then my cell phone rang. It was a member of our group, calling to tell me that she would be bringing a friend for whom we'd been praying. I told her how great it was to hear this news and that I'd see her there in less than an hour.

When I hung up the phone, I wondered why I had just said what I did., Then God reminded me of John 15:13 and that at least one or two of the other members of my group were tired too, but they'd be there and so would a first-time guest.

During our time of worship, I asked God to renew my energy and give me what I needed to be an active part of the discussion and ministry that would follow. To my surprise, He did! After the meeting, I had a chance to talk with our visitor and connect with him in a meaningful way. On the way home, Etna asked me why I was so wound up. I could only say, "It was God. I had no energy when I walked into that house tonight."

That night, I slept like a log and woke up totally refreshed, just as if I'd been in bed for an extra hour or two. By going to that meeting and making our visitor a priority, God supplied my need.

Remember the illustration of the jar and the rocks, pebbles, sand, and water? Being an active member of my small group is a big rock in my jar, or a major priority in life. Rest was a pebble, which God gave me at the appropriate time.

A Lifestyle Of Outreach

For many Christians, the word "church" brings up all kinds of inaccurate images or hurts from the past. They might have been raised in a church that was legalistic or judgmental. Or, the members of their church gossiped about them or didn't show them the unconditional love of God.

You have the opportunity to introduce your small group members to friends and co-workers who have had bad experiences in the past. When you're at work or with unchurched friends, tell them about your good friends from your small group as often as possible! Describe how the relationships you've formed are based on trust, confidentiality, and a desire to find the love of God. There are millions of people in our world who grew up in the church and think it has no relevance to their lives.

While I was visiting a church to help them with some small group leader training, a small group leader and a couple of his members took me to lunch. When the waitress came up to our table, the small group leader greeted her by name because he made it a point to eat there once a week with his wife and kids. She asked about his family and talked for a minute or two, then took our order.

When she came back to the table to bring us our food, the leader said, "Hey, if you knew that there was a group of people who really cared about each other and would love to meet you, would you be interested?"

She smiled and said, "Any friend of yours is a friend of mine."

The leader introduced the couple from his group that was with us at the table, and asked her what night she had off that next week. Right then and there, they decided to have her and her son over for dinner, and she said yes!

Her comment was funny. She said "I've been serving you food for months. It's about time you served me something to eat!"

This is reaching out! It's making friends with people you interact with each day and extending an opportunity to form a deeper friendship with them by including them in your circle.

People who won't walk into a church building will come to your small group meeting or over to your house for a barbeque or a party. In your small group, the environment is designed for God's people to share transparently, receive ministry, and see God operate among them in a special way. The world will discover how intimately God wants to relate to them by being around you and your small group.

Life Goes On

If you will work to incorporate the principles I've shared in this book, you and your small group will grow and continue to be a healthy expression of God's people.

As it grows, you'll have the opportunity to help the new people coming in, which for me has been exciting. It helps me discover new things about God and myself.

One day, you will be ready to move out of your current spiritual home and begin a family of your own. Don't be apprehensive or scared of this. It's just the next natural step in maturity as a believer who lives in biblical community.

Just remember this and you'll be just fine: We are ordinary people who serve an extra-ordinary God. If you leave God out of the equation, your mind will be filled with reasons as to why you can't be a small group member who is involved, who serves, and who loves those who are not yet inside your circle. Include God in the mix, and it all looks possible!

My hope for you is that your small group will not be a once-a-week meeting where you go, you talk, and then you go away until the next week. It ____ ____re! May it be a life-changing experience for you, the other members of your group, and everyone with whom you come in contact!